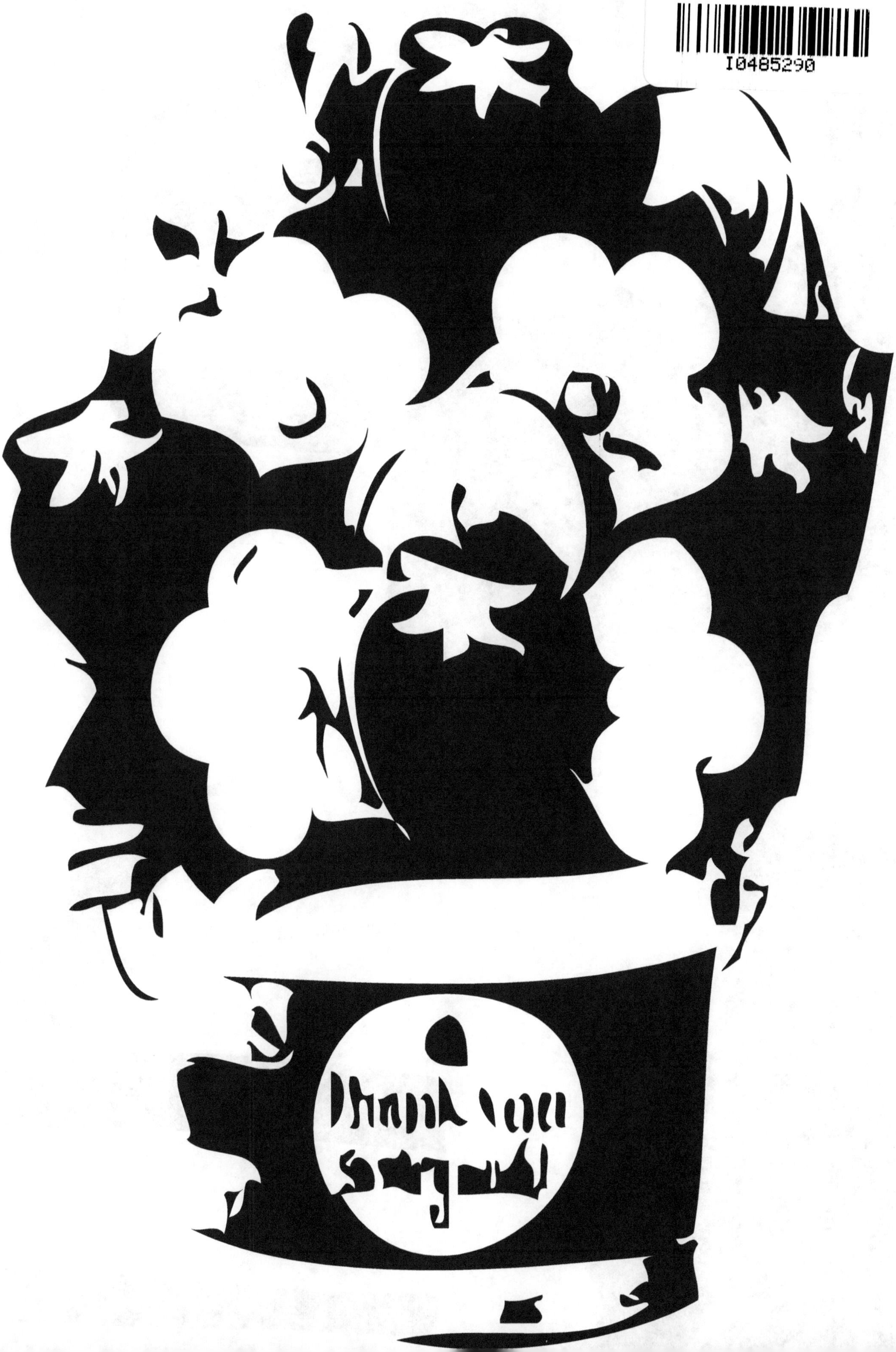

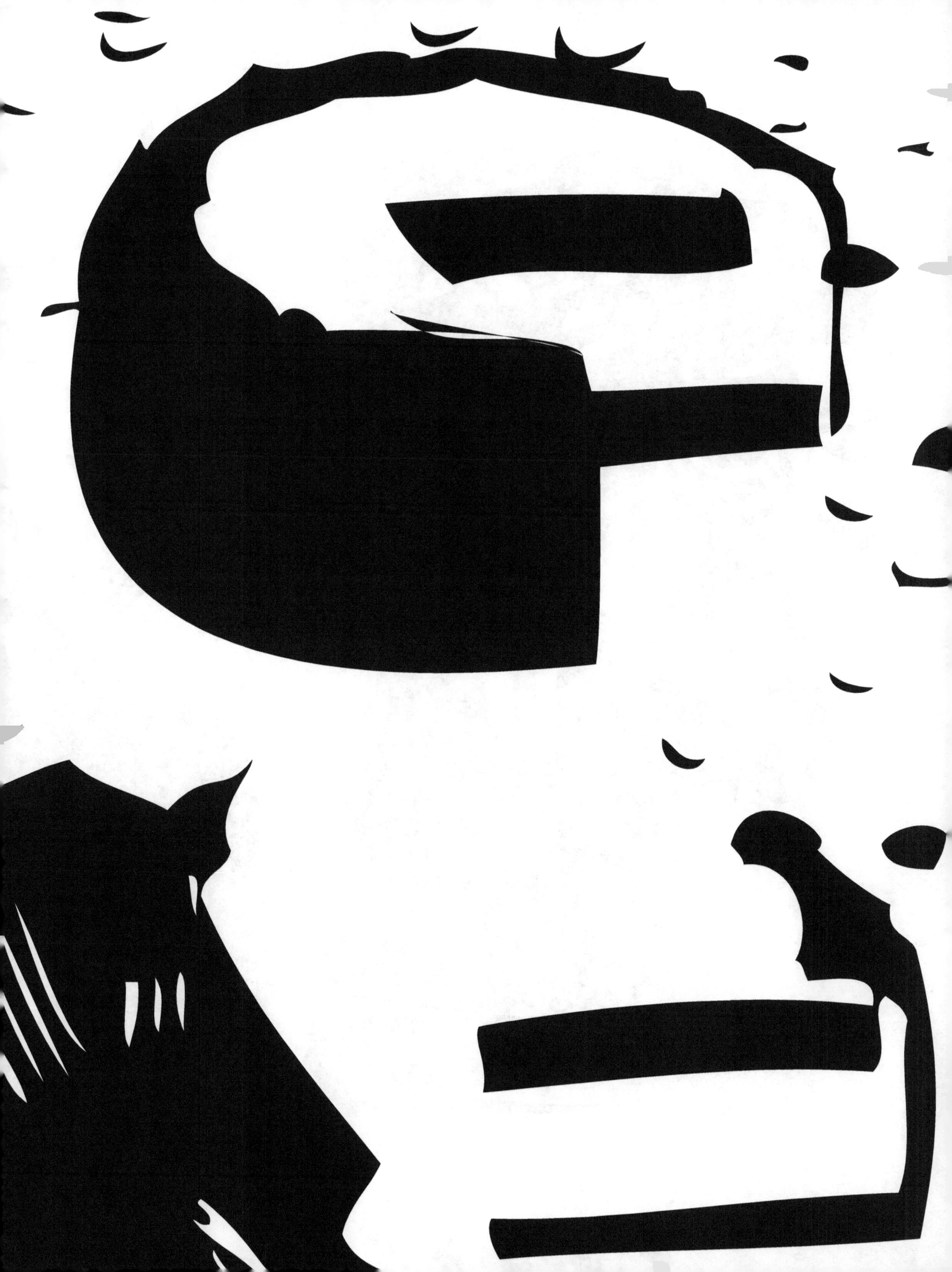

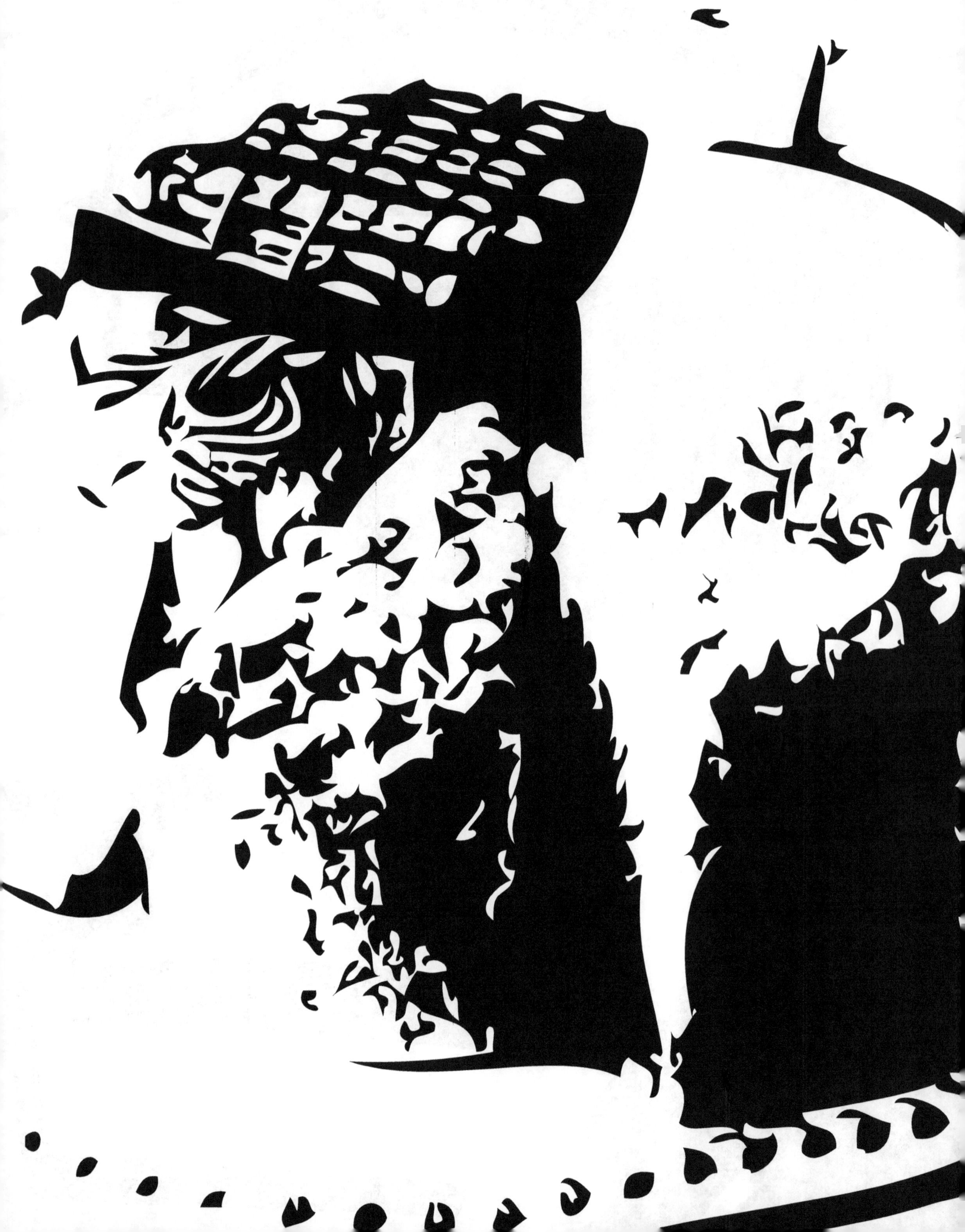

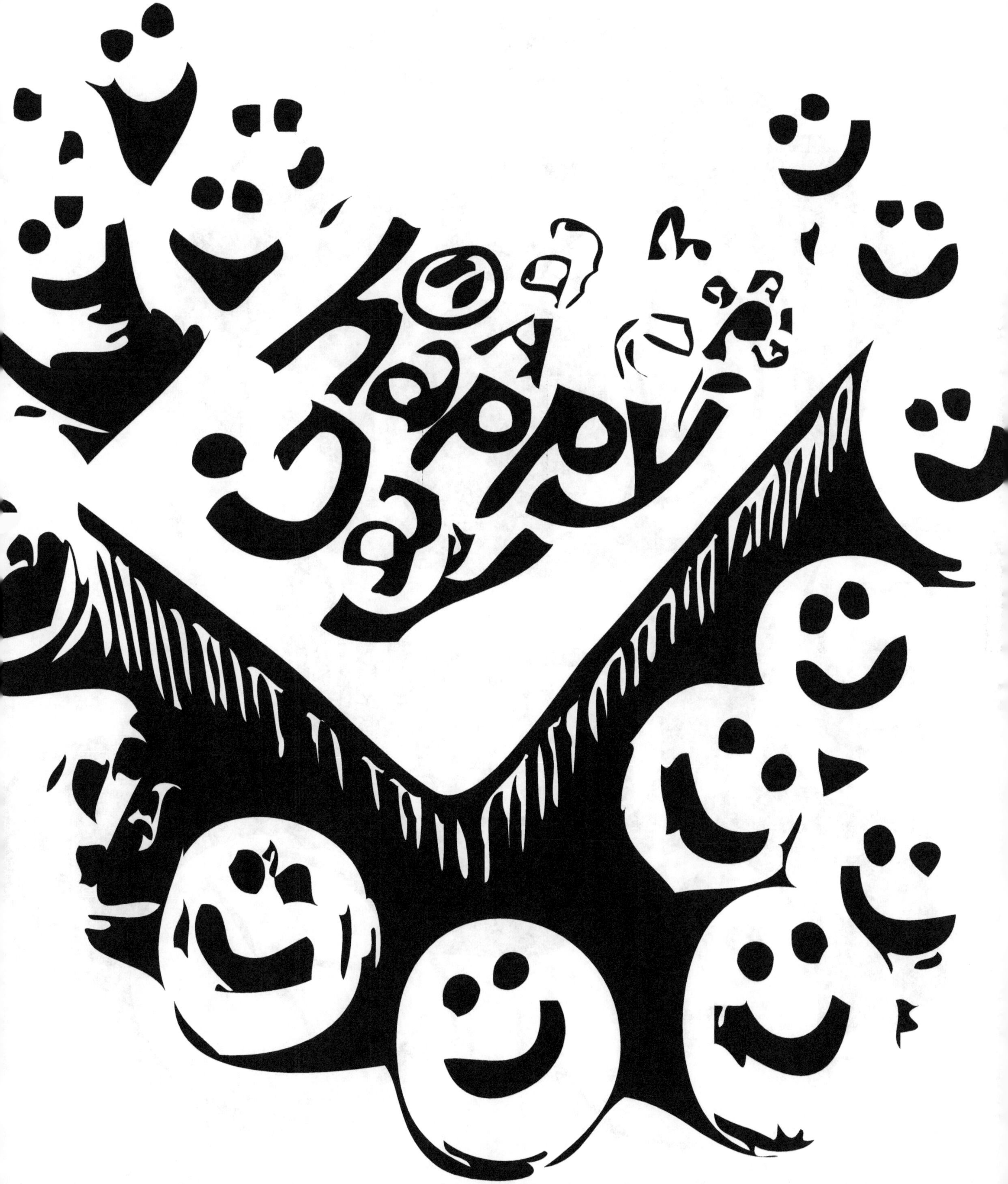
Happy

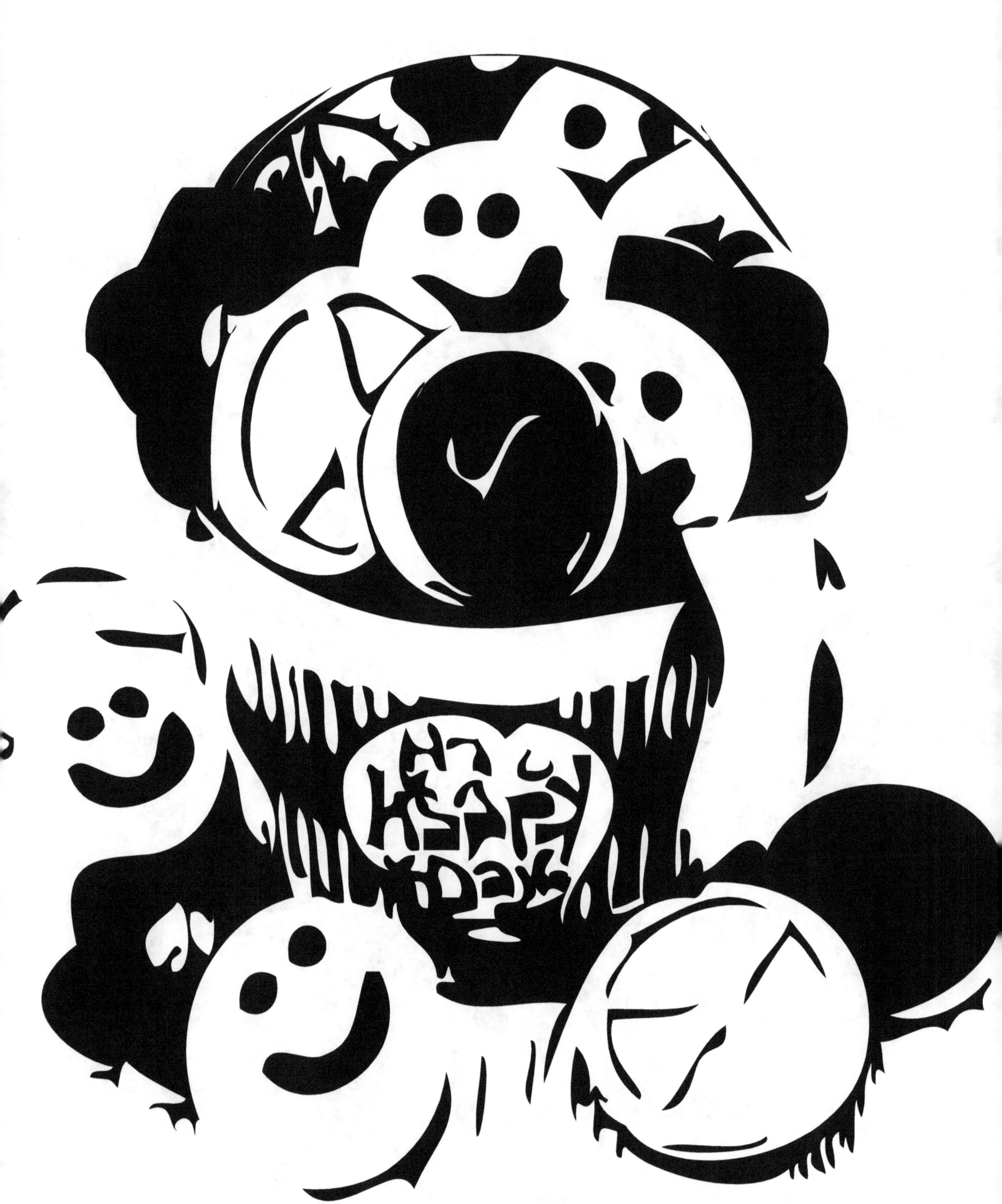

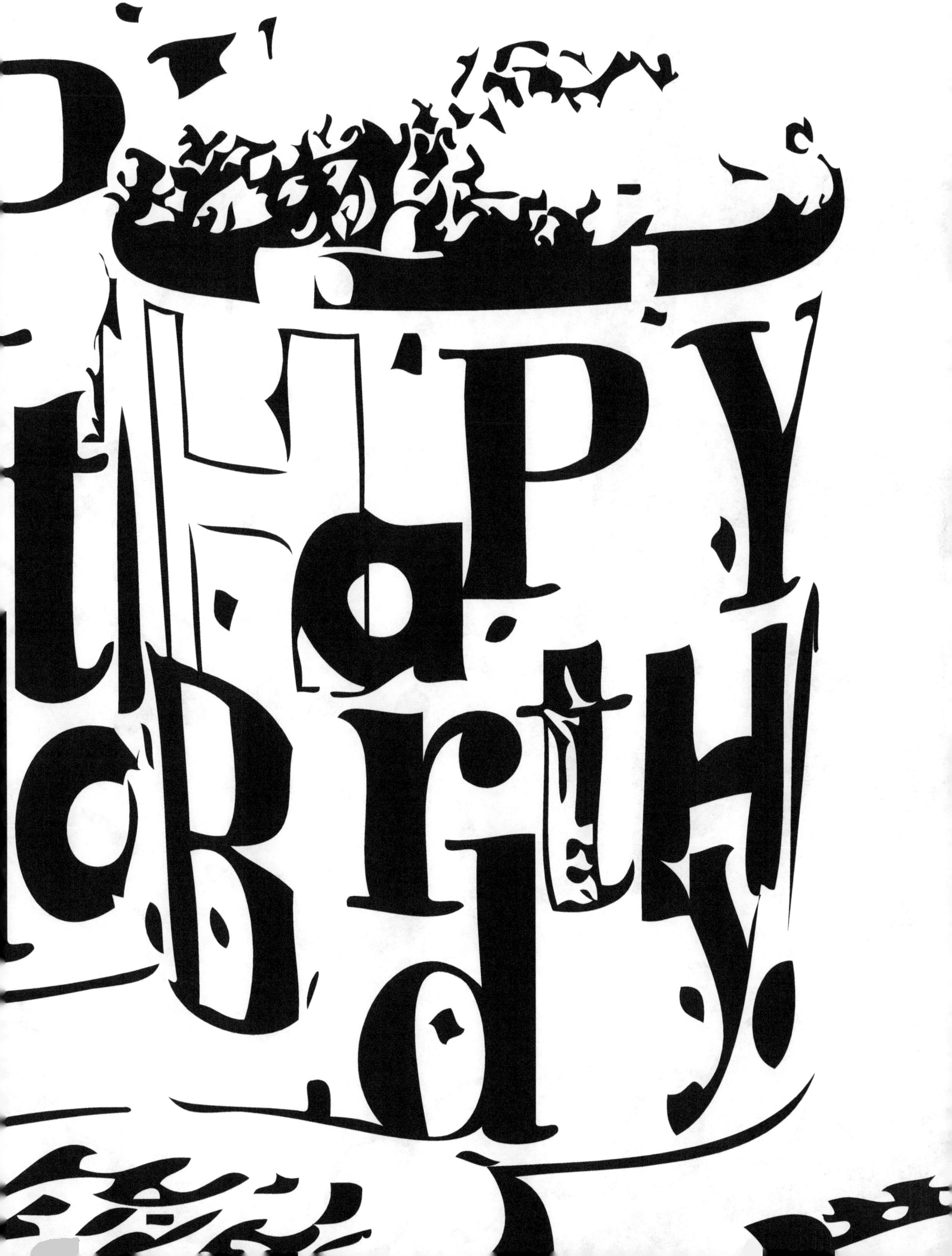

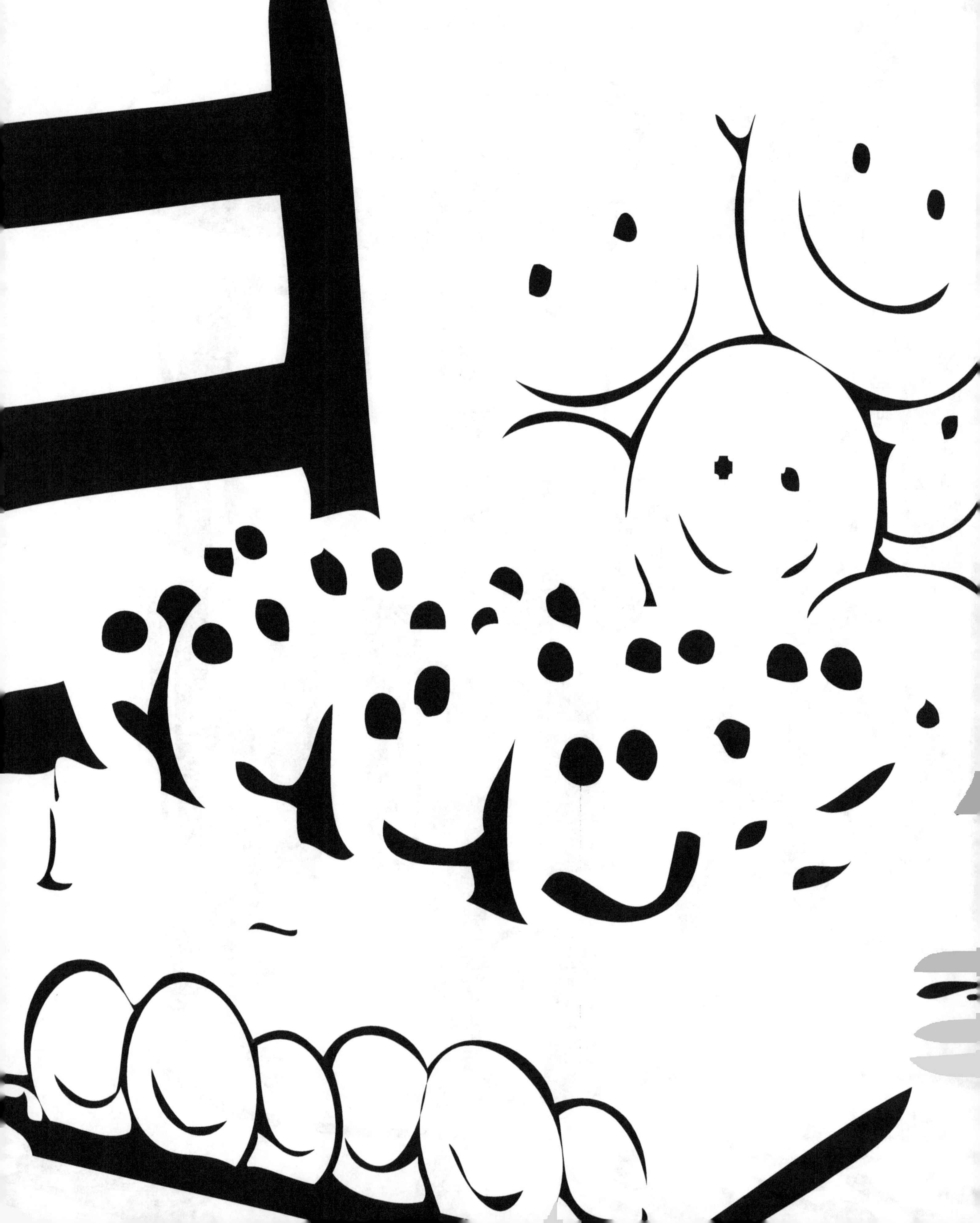

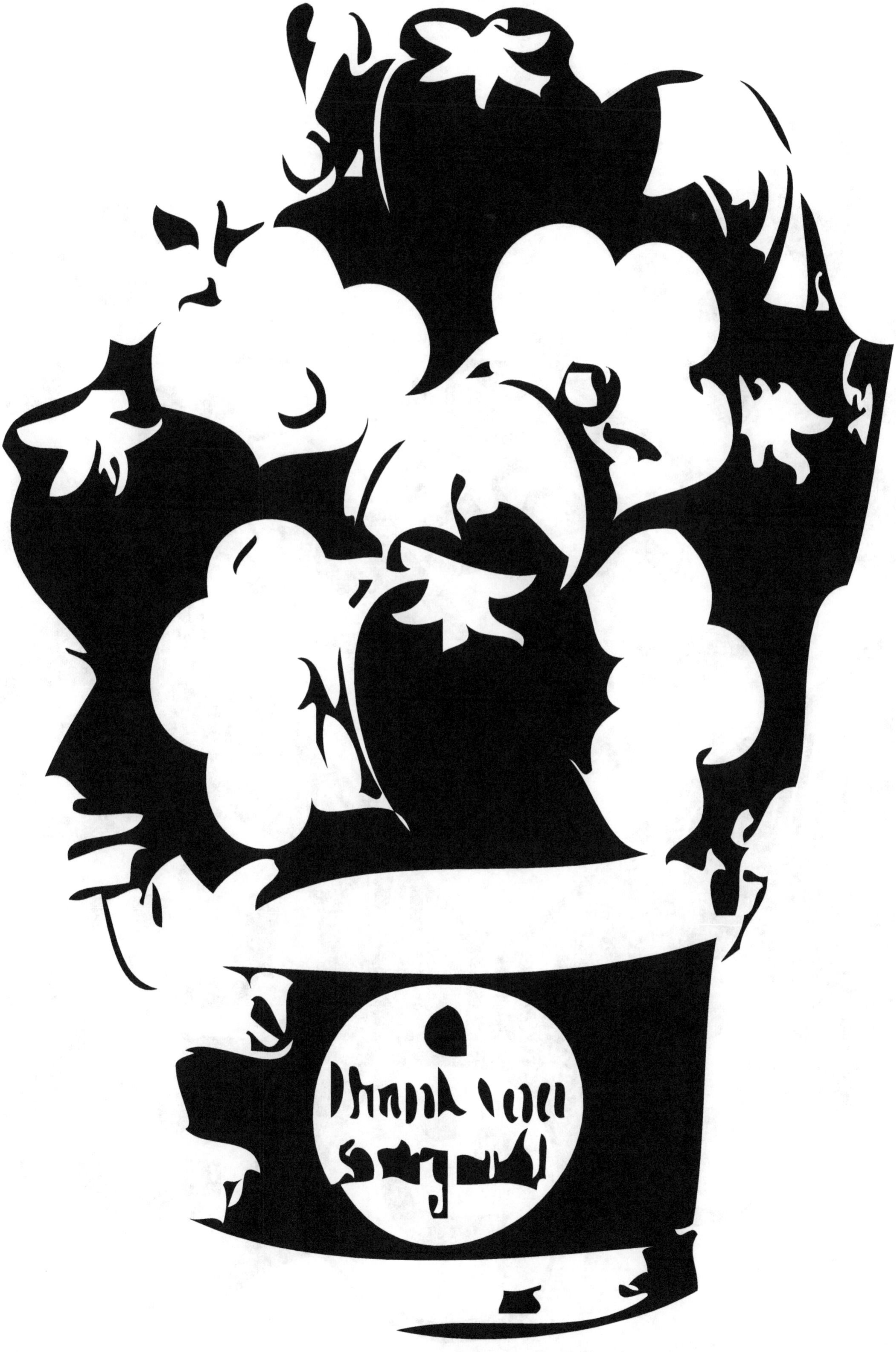

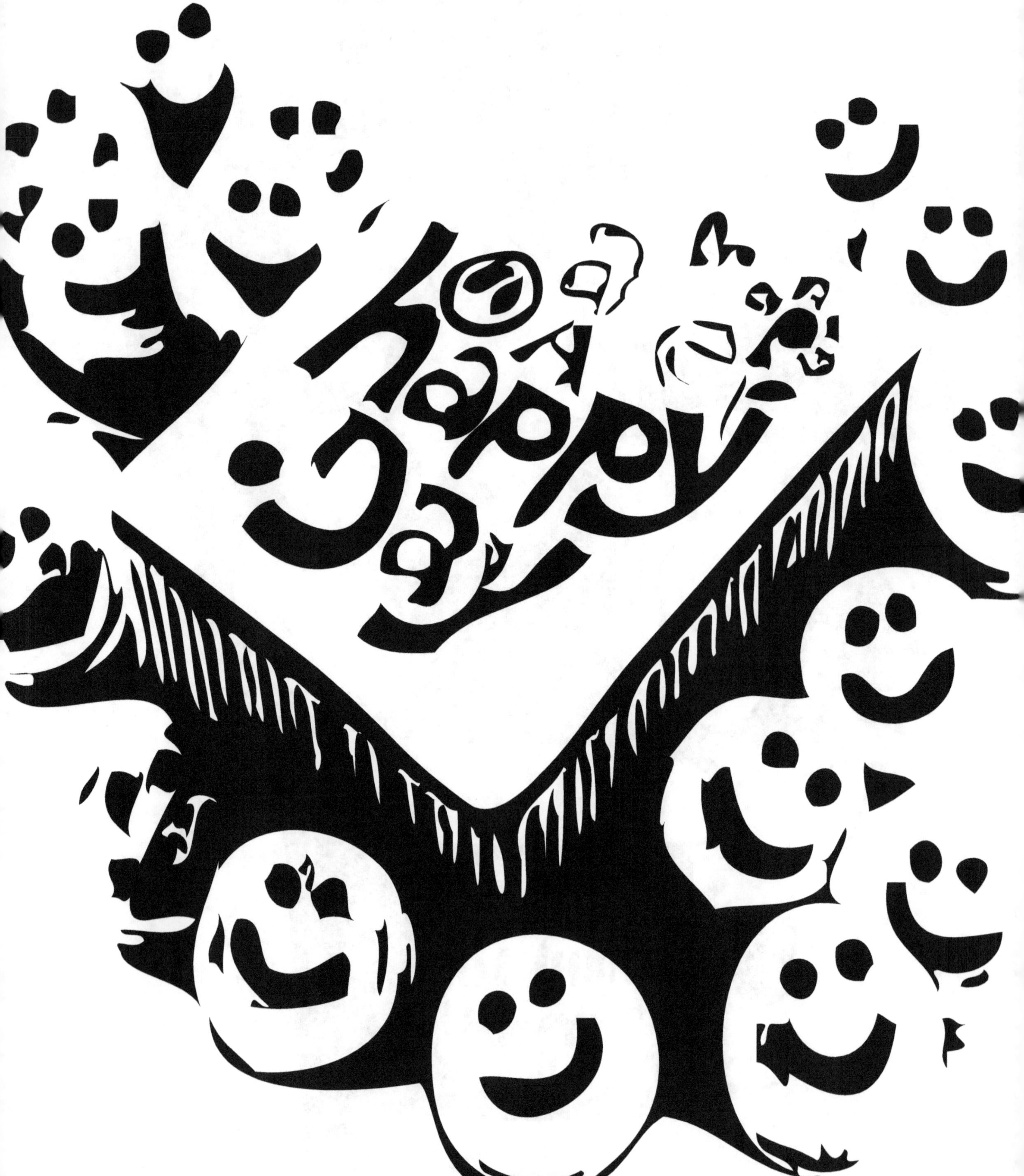
happy day

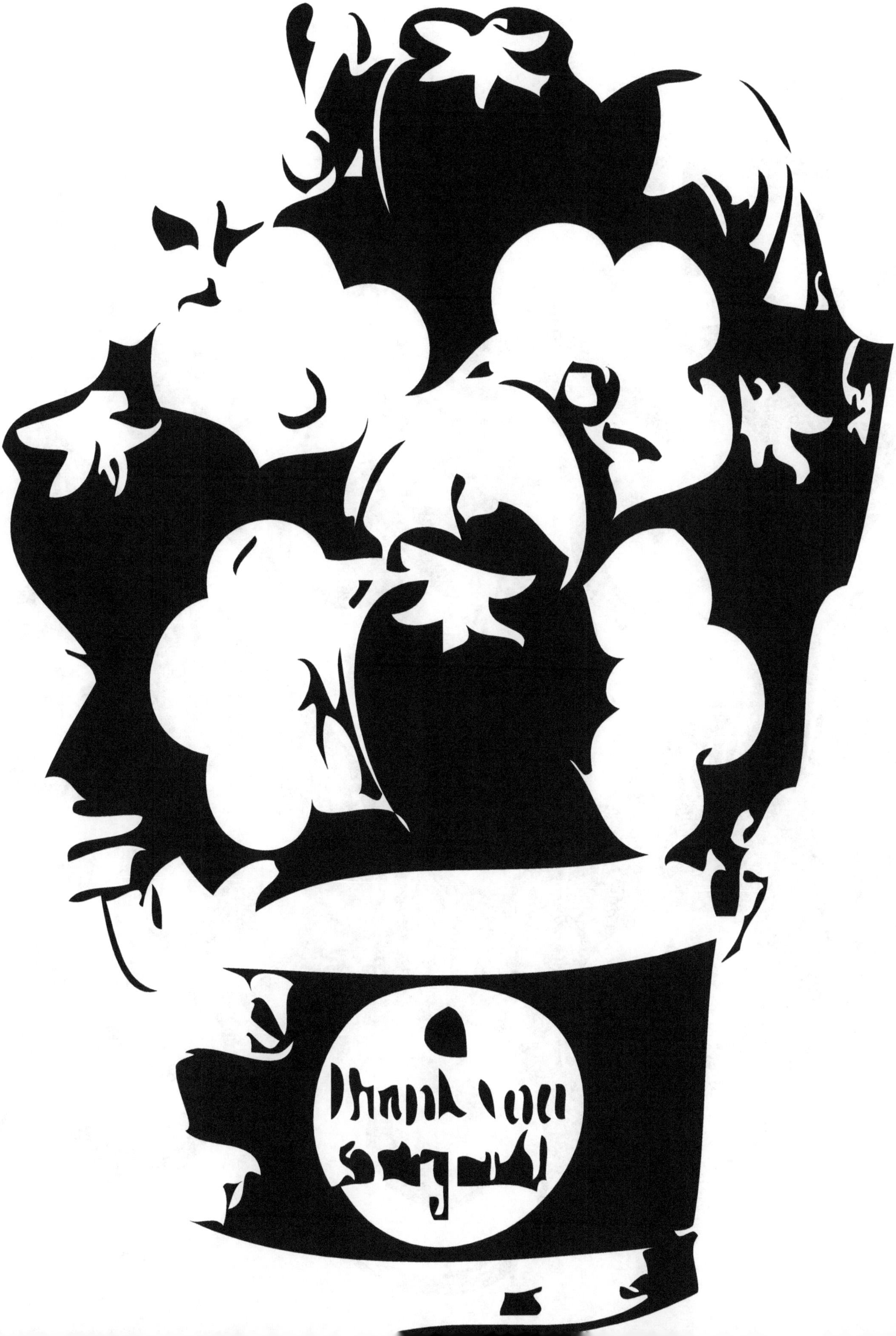

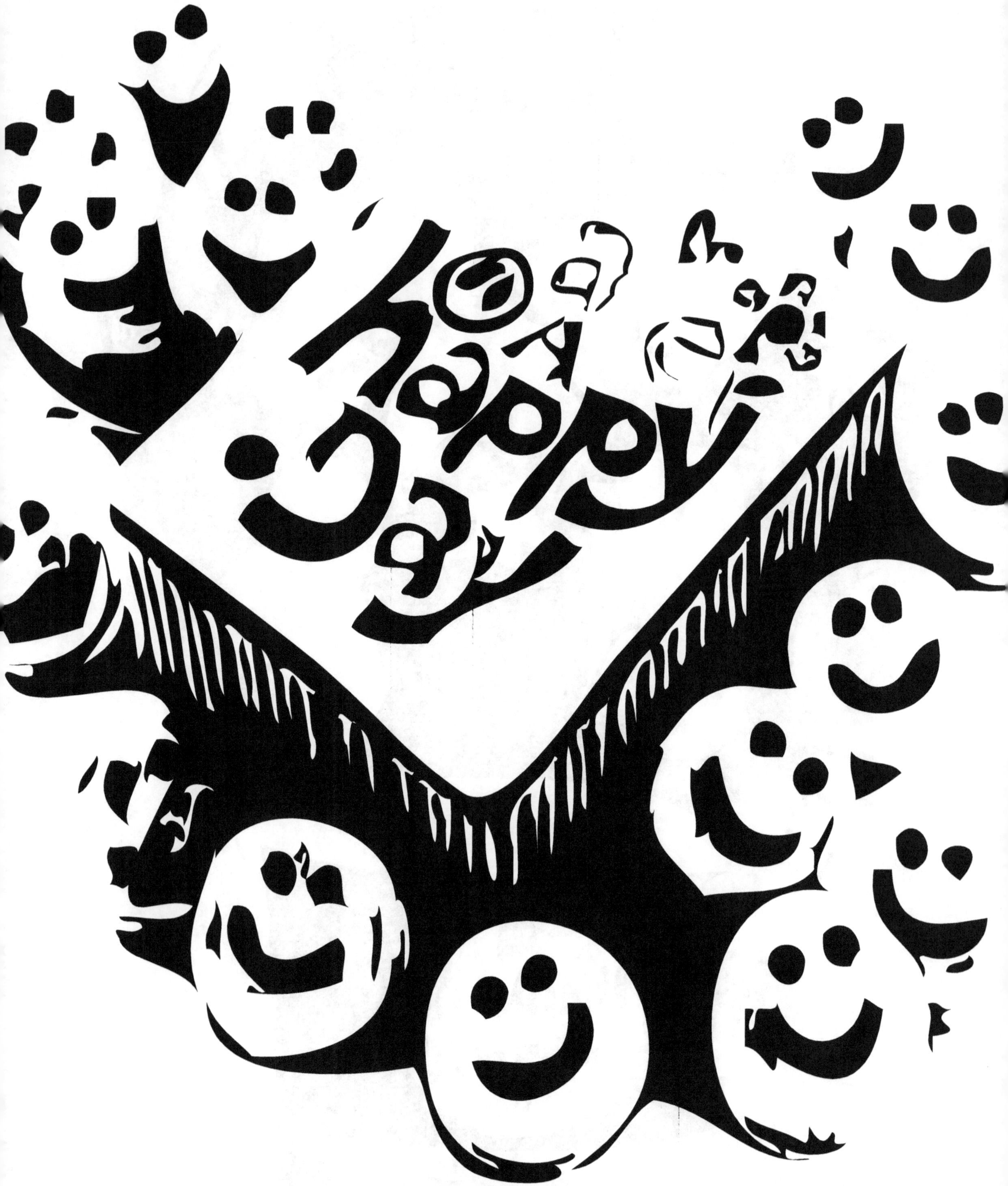
Happy Day

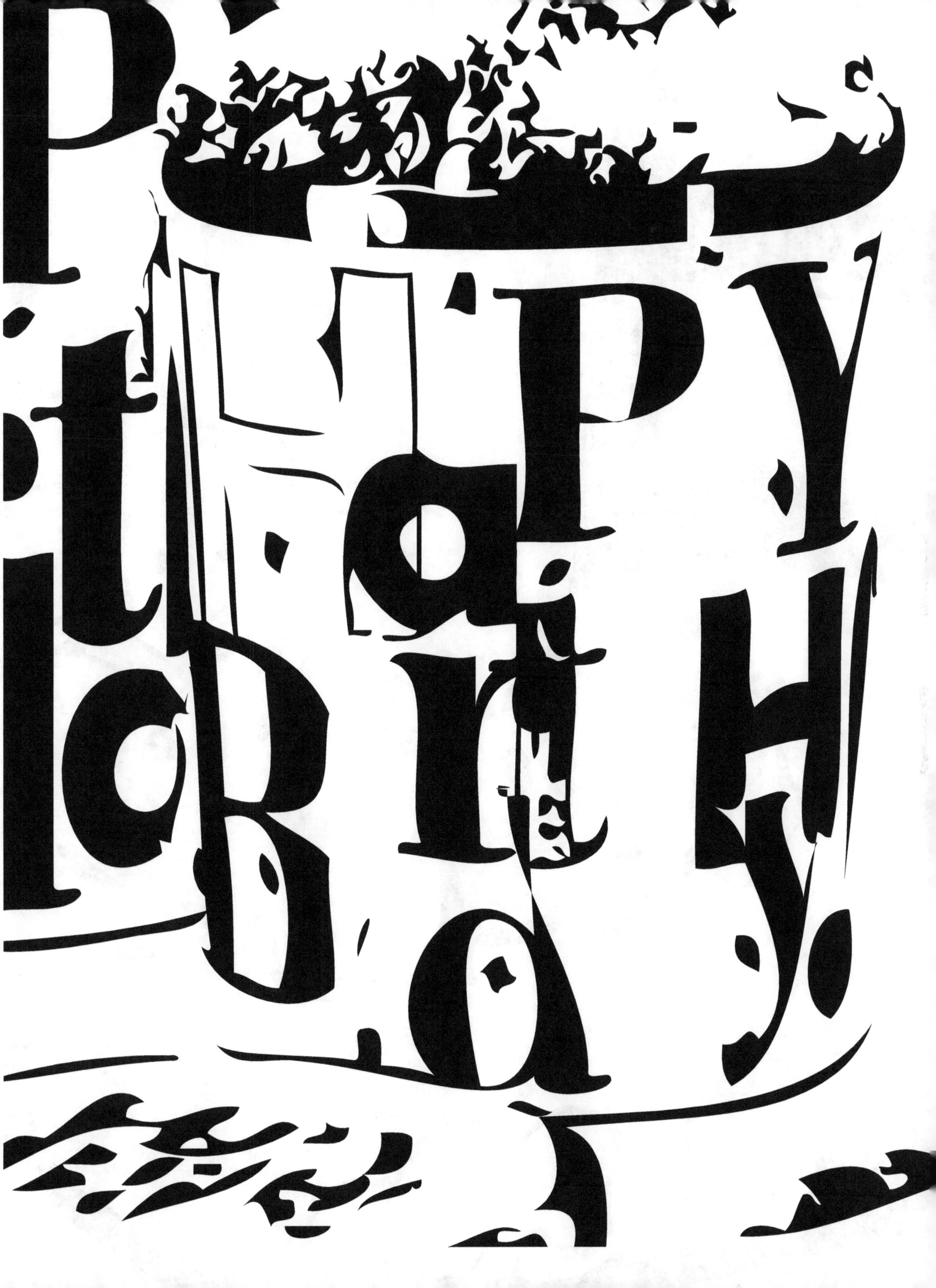

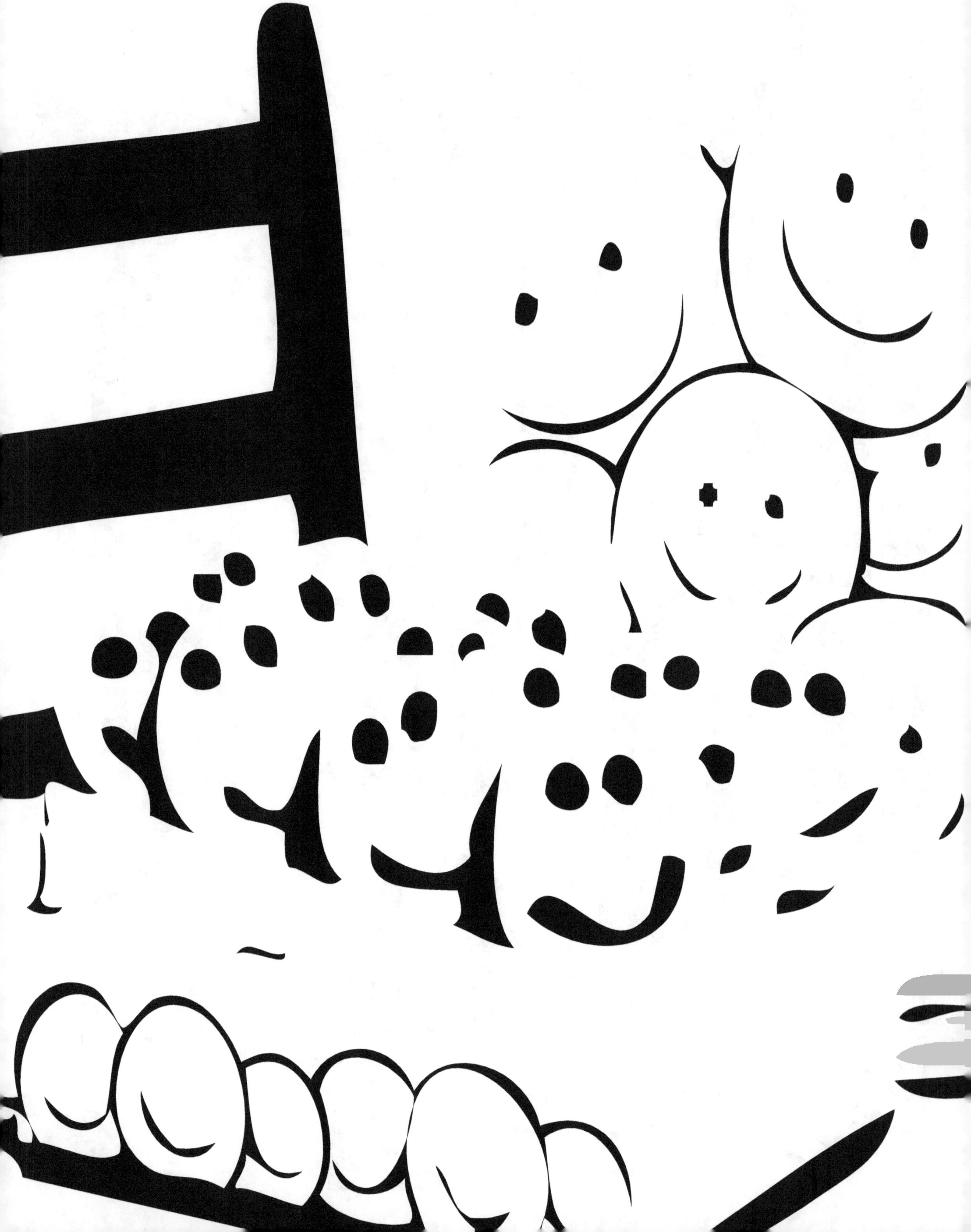

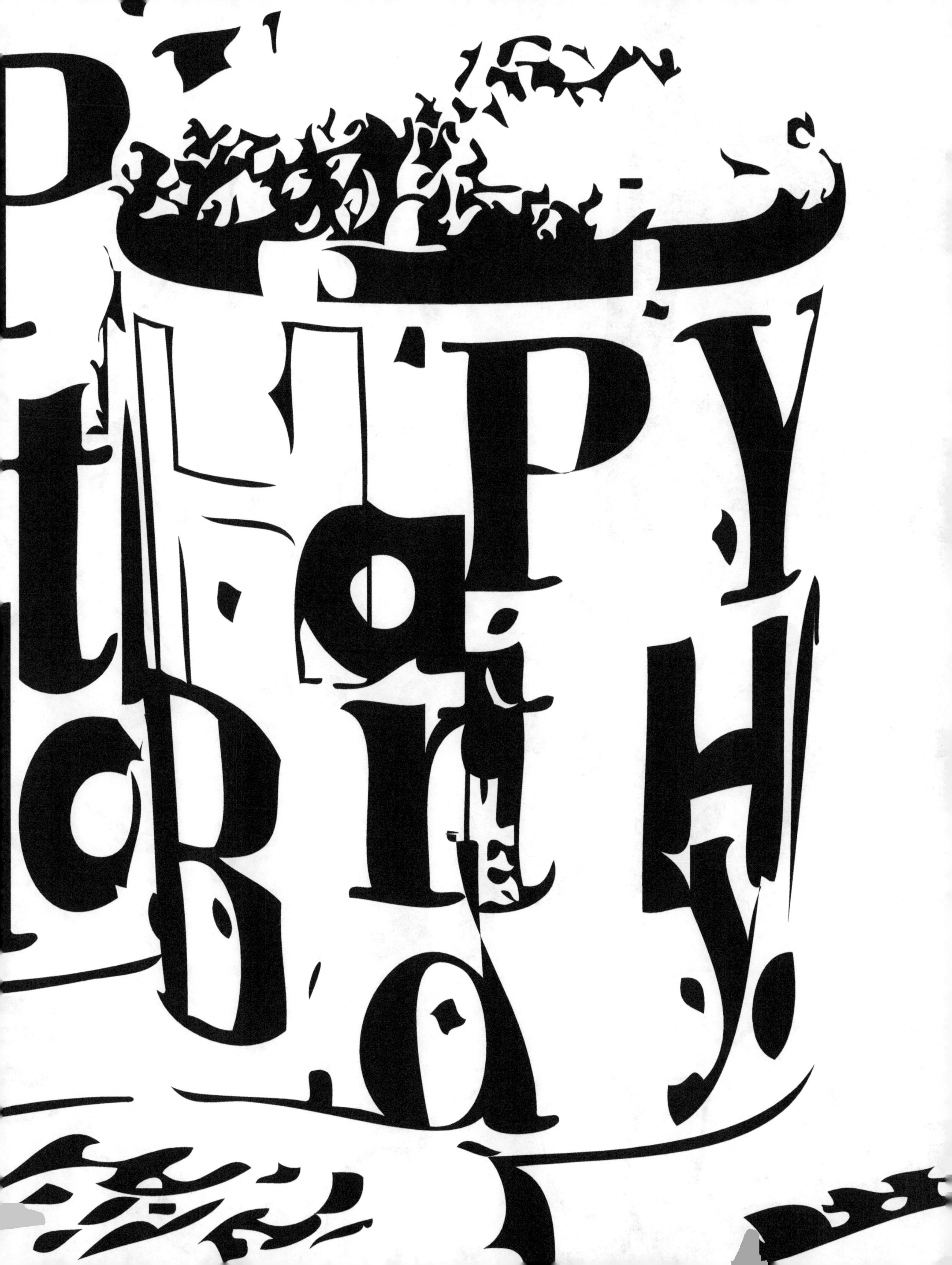

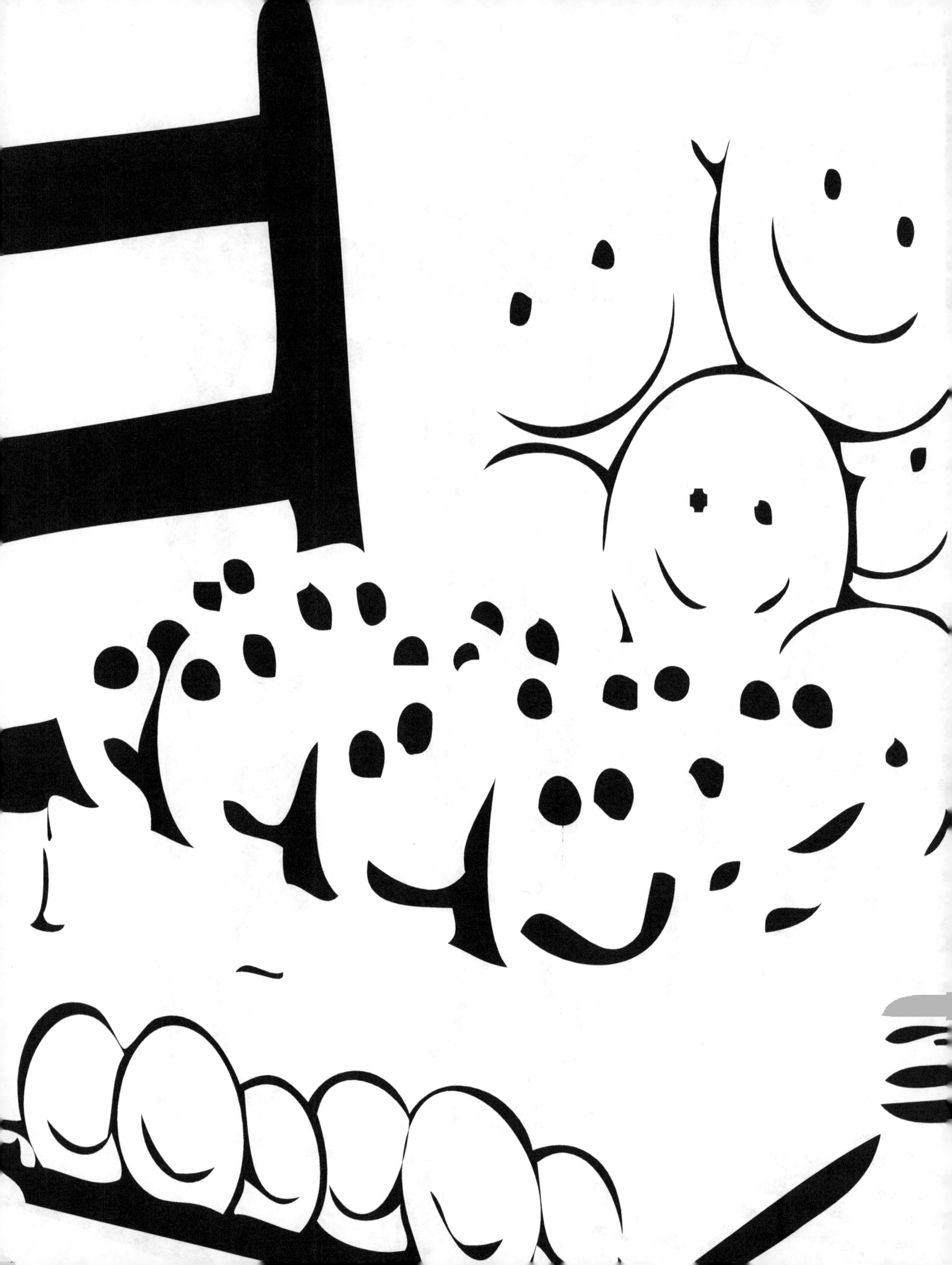

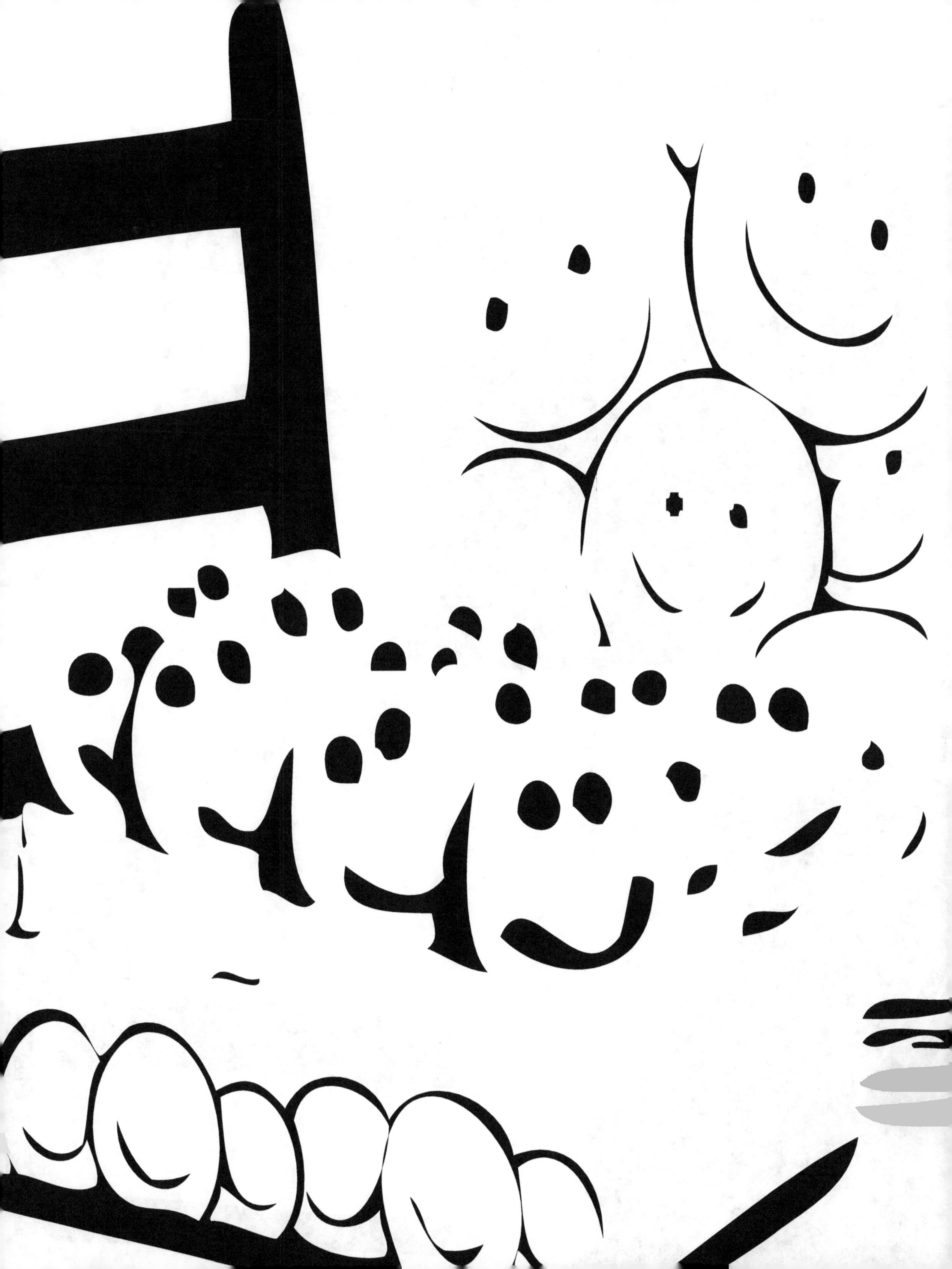

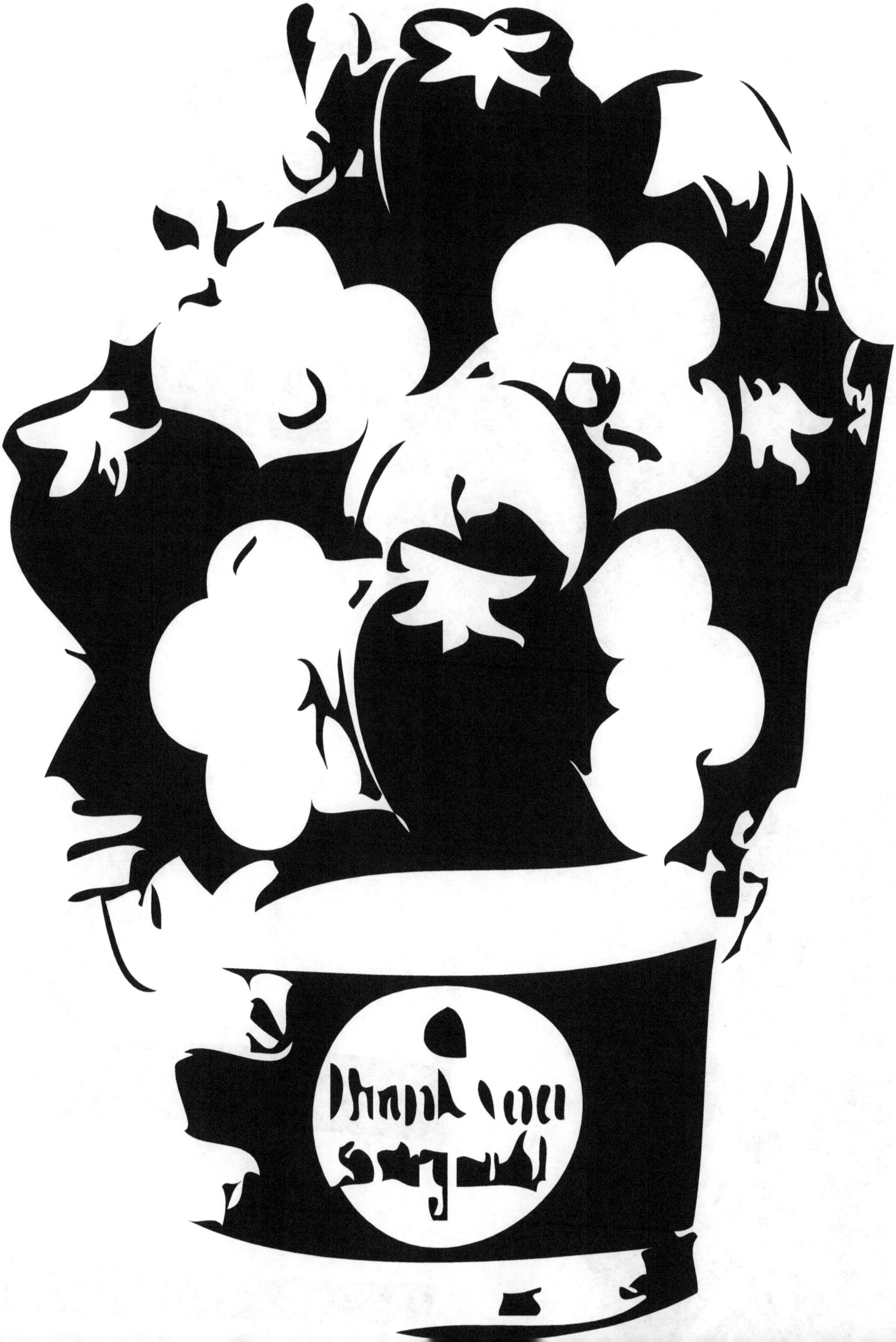

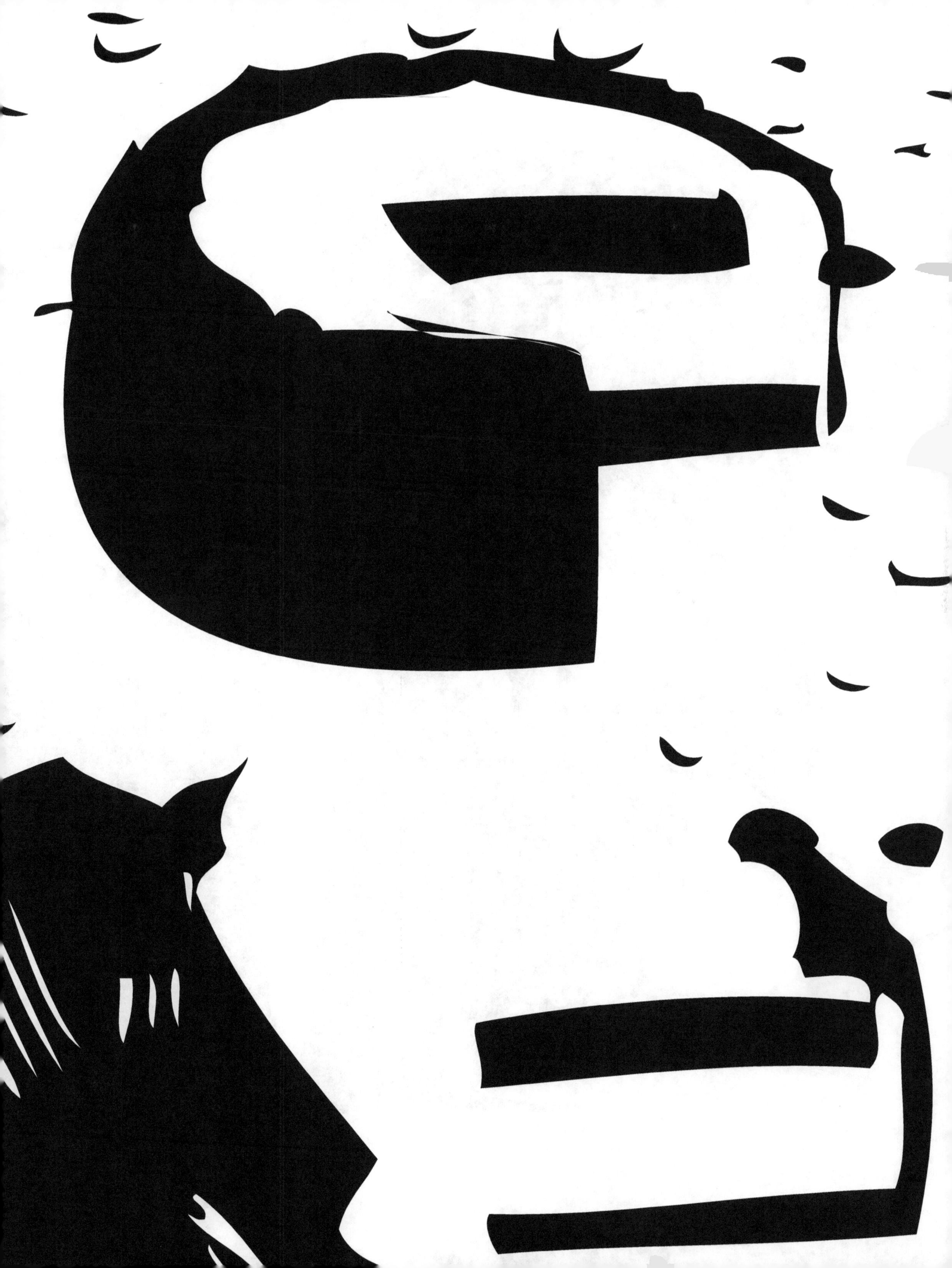

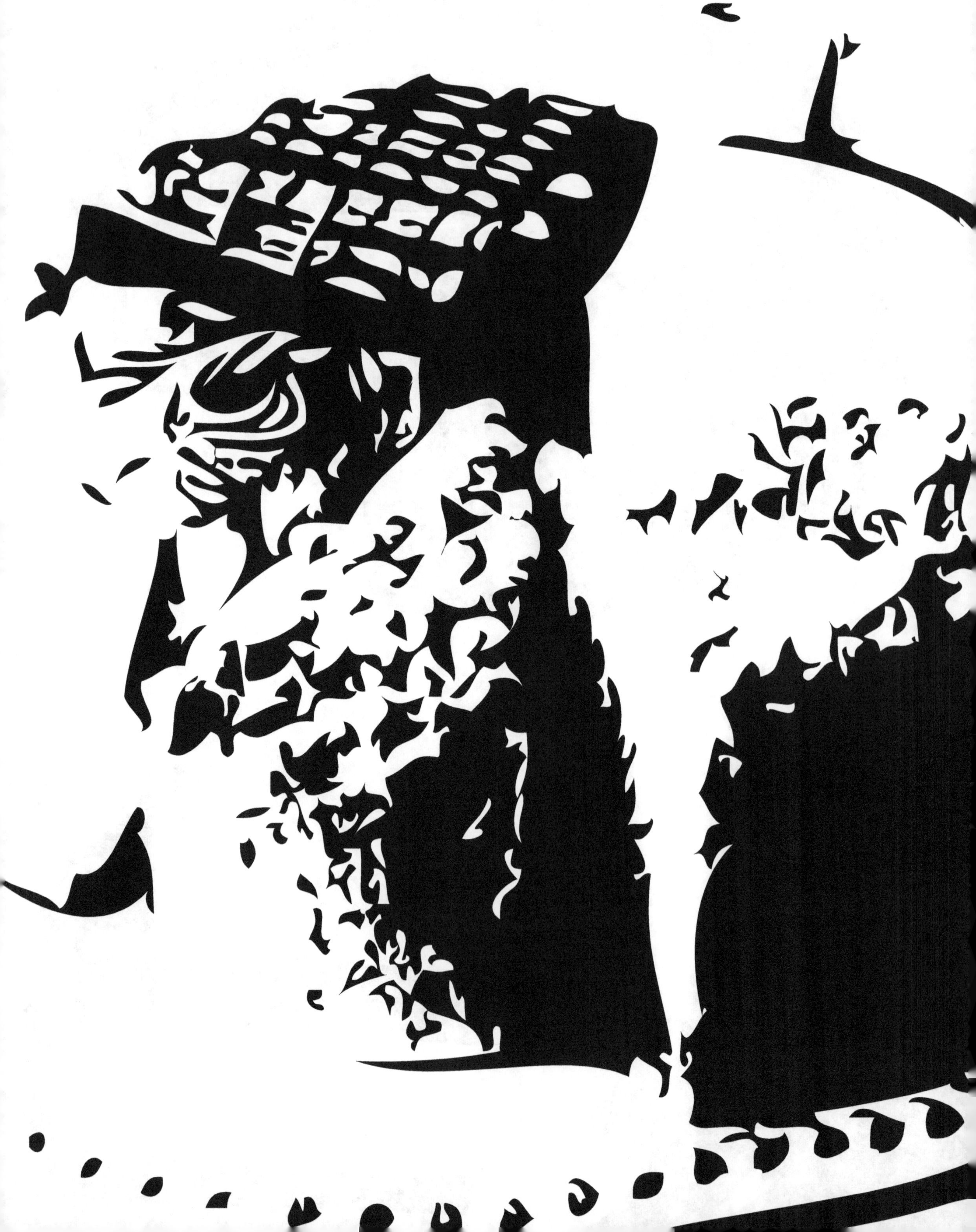

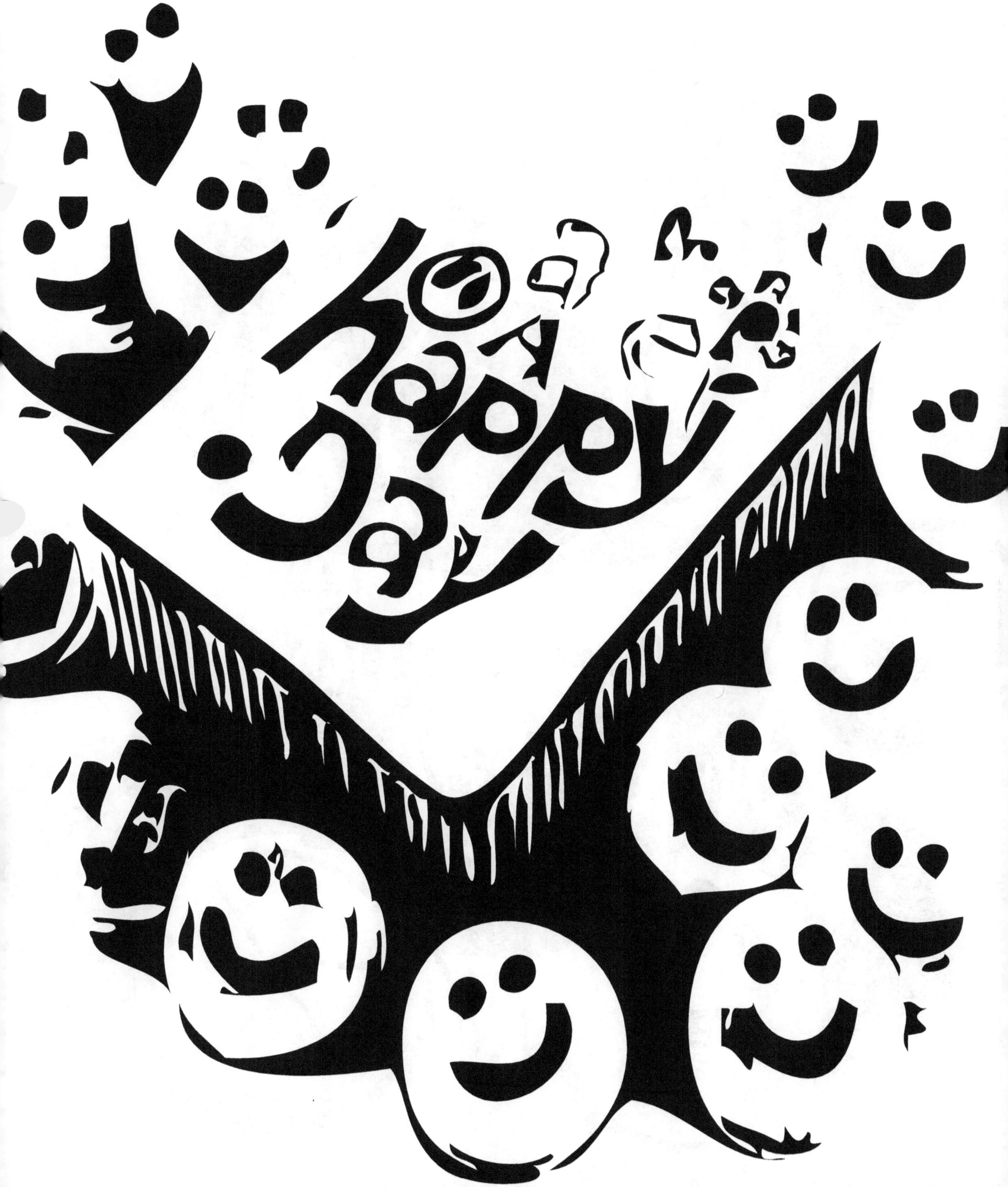

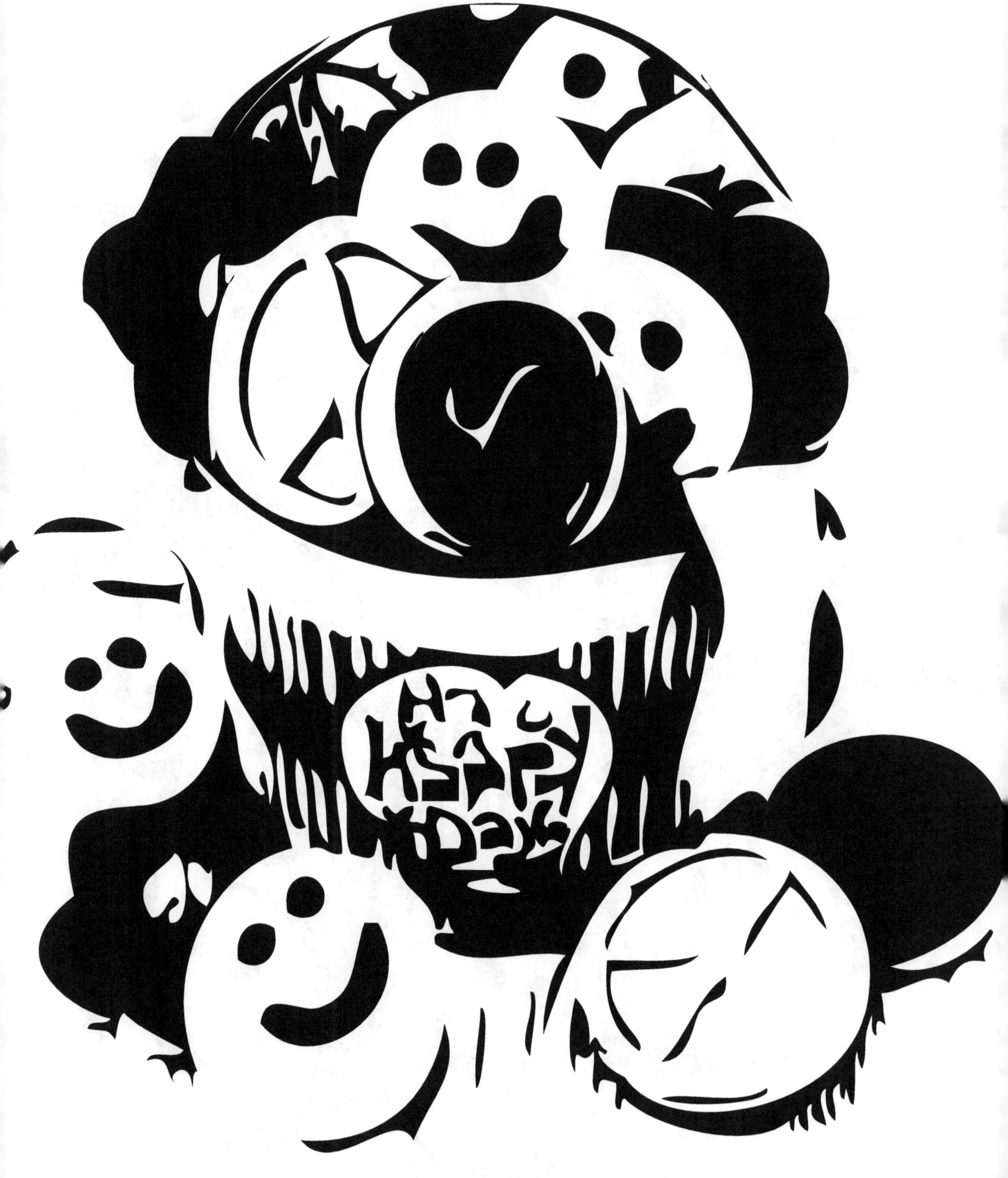

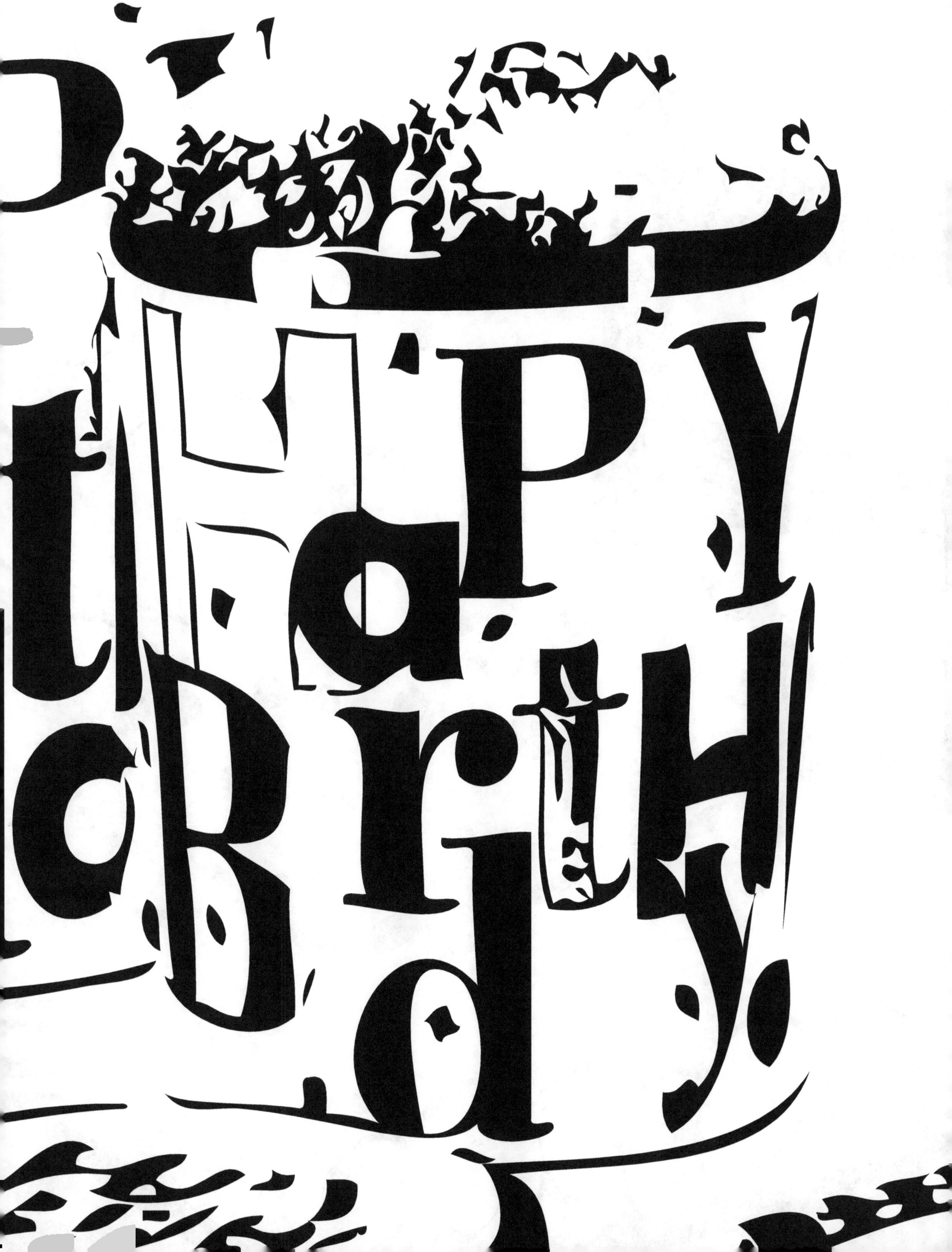

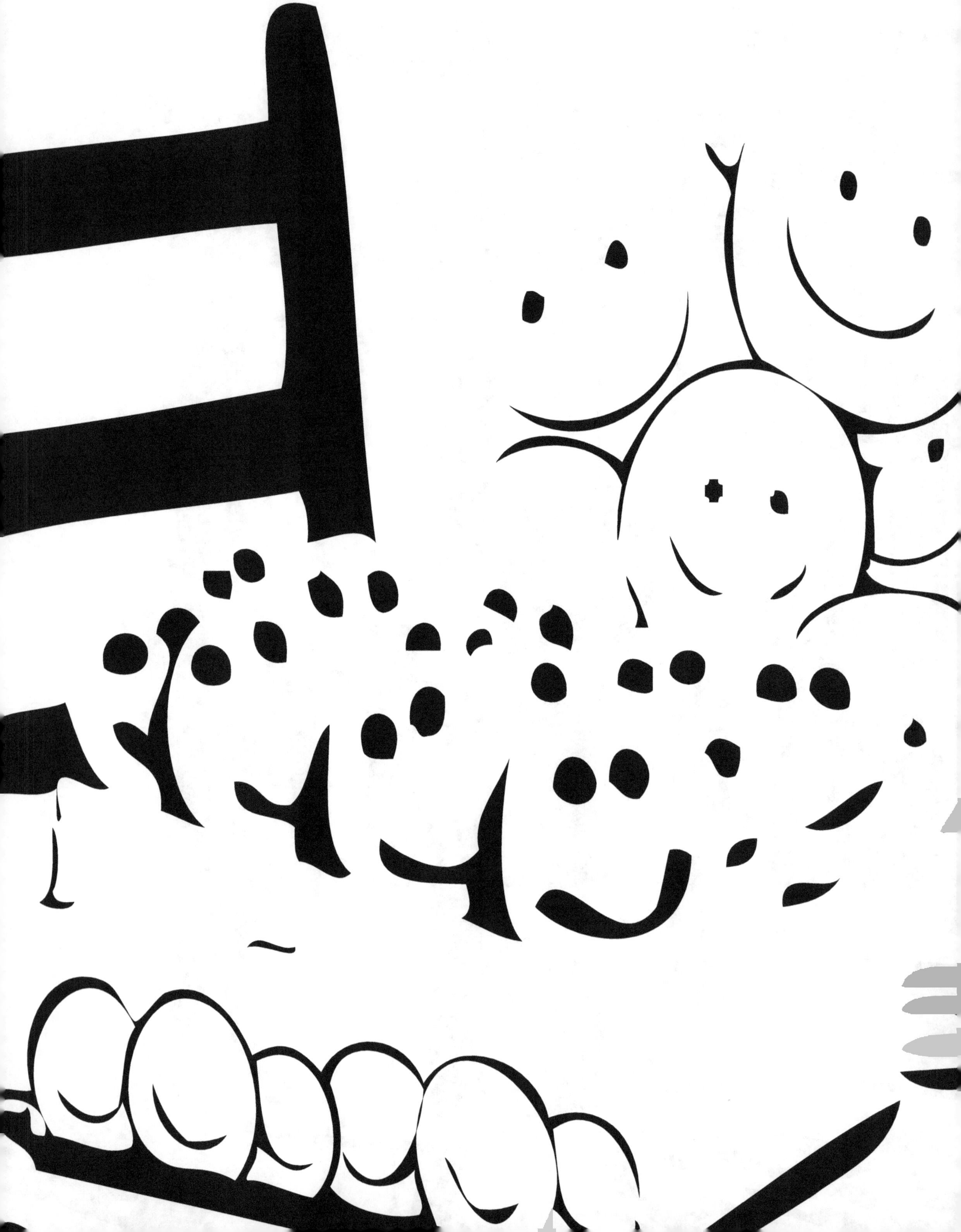

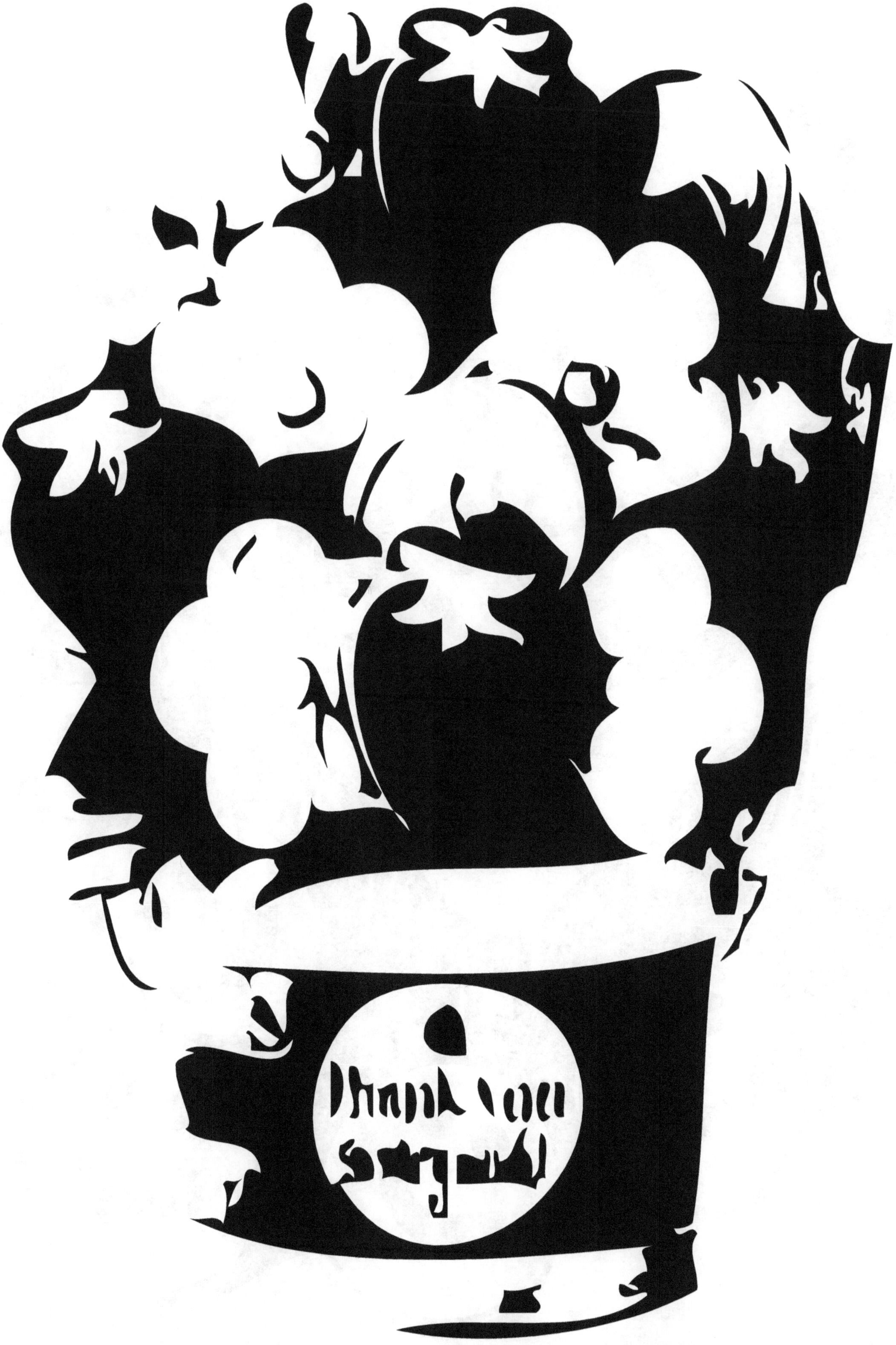

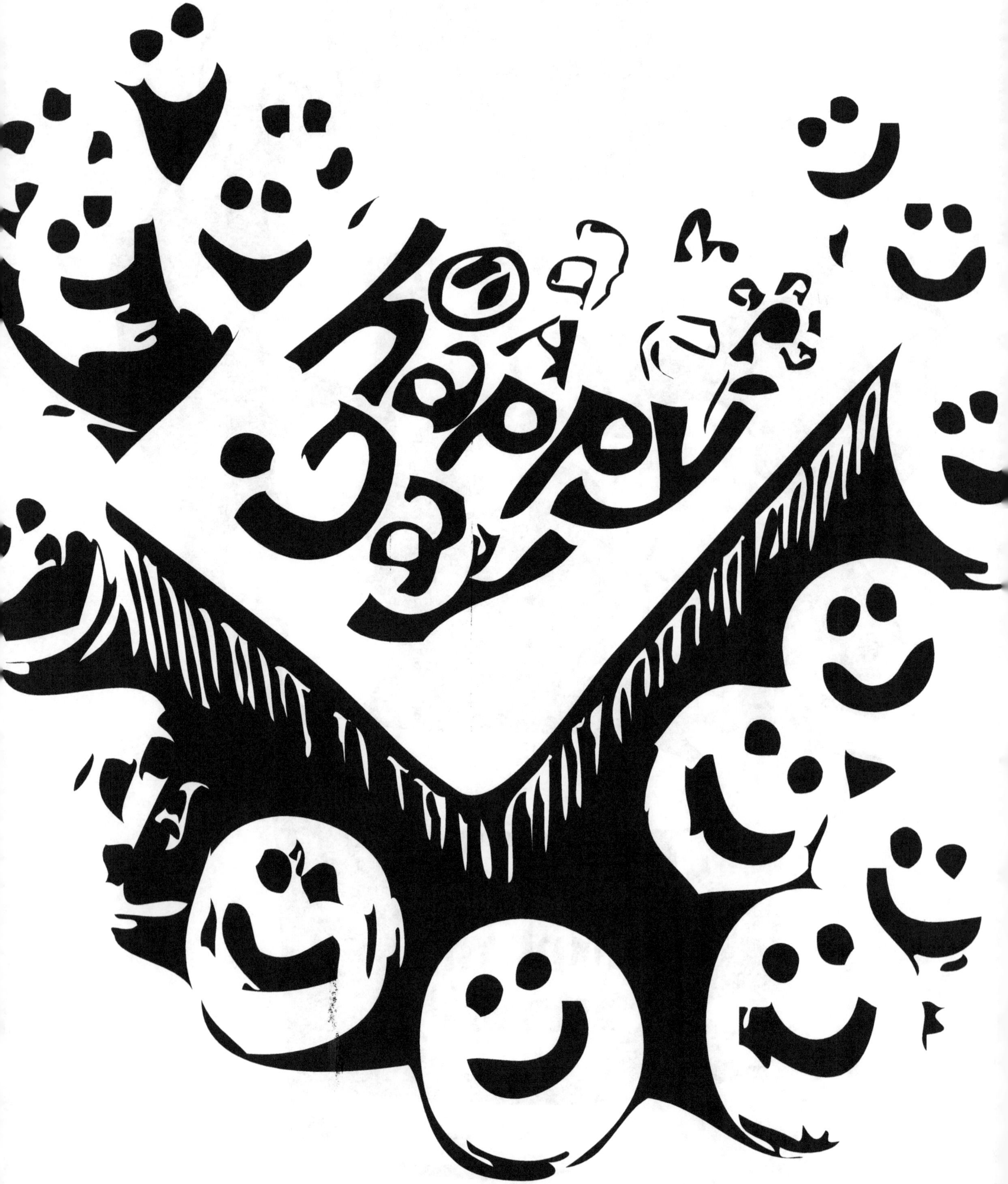
Oh Happy Day

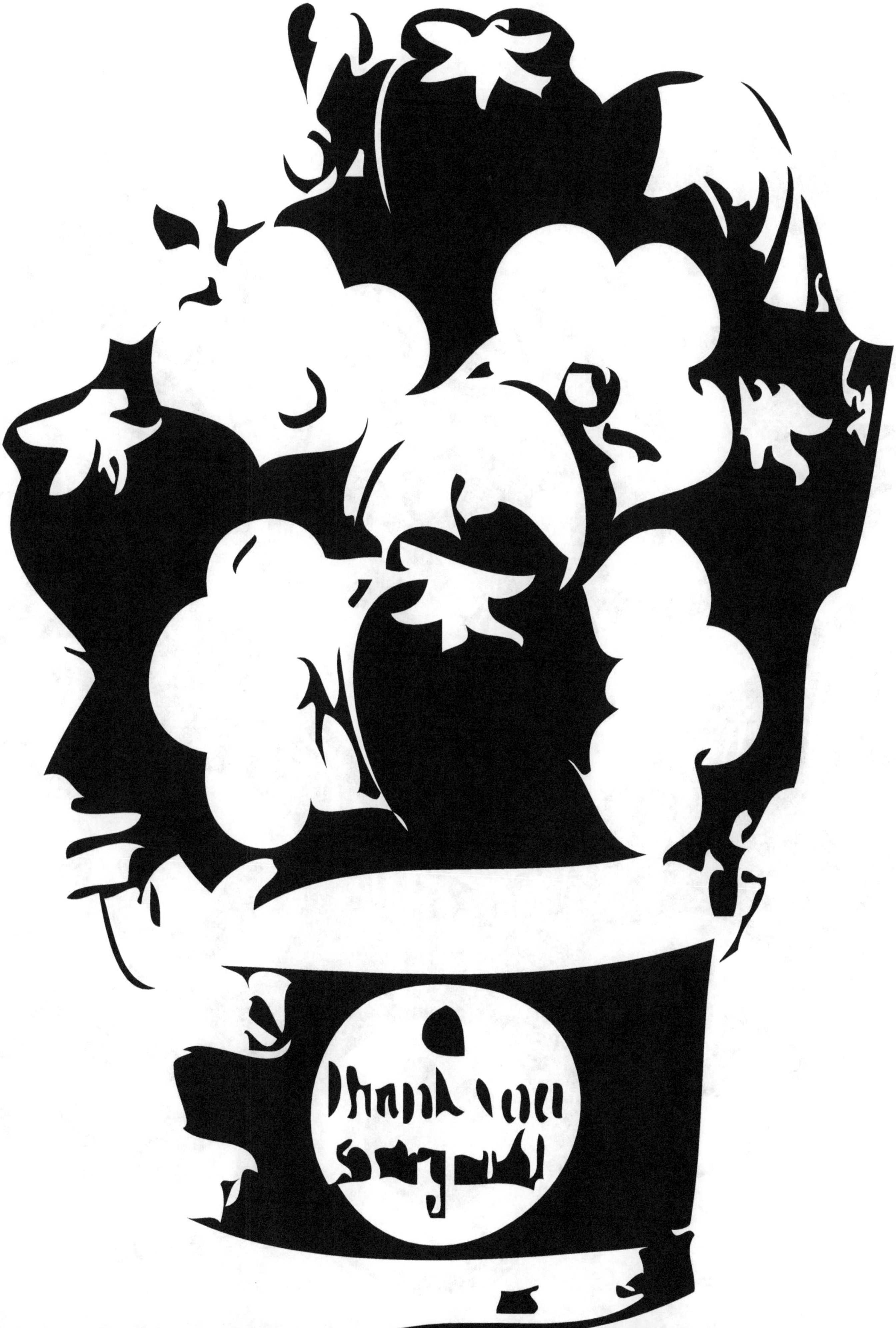

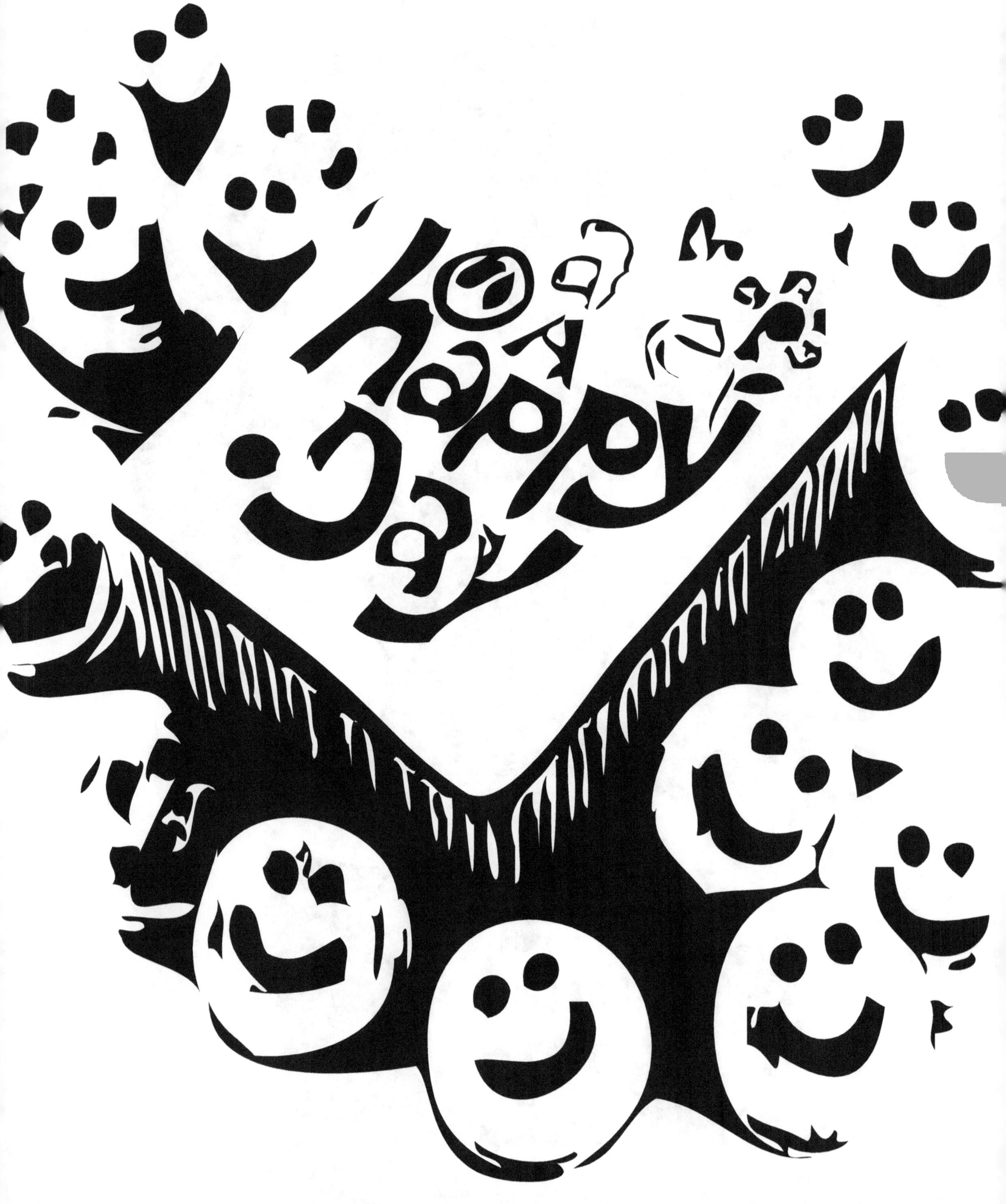
Have A happy Day

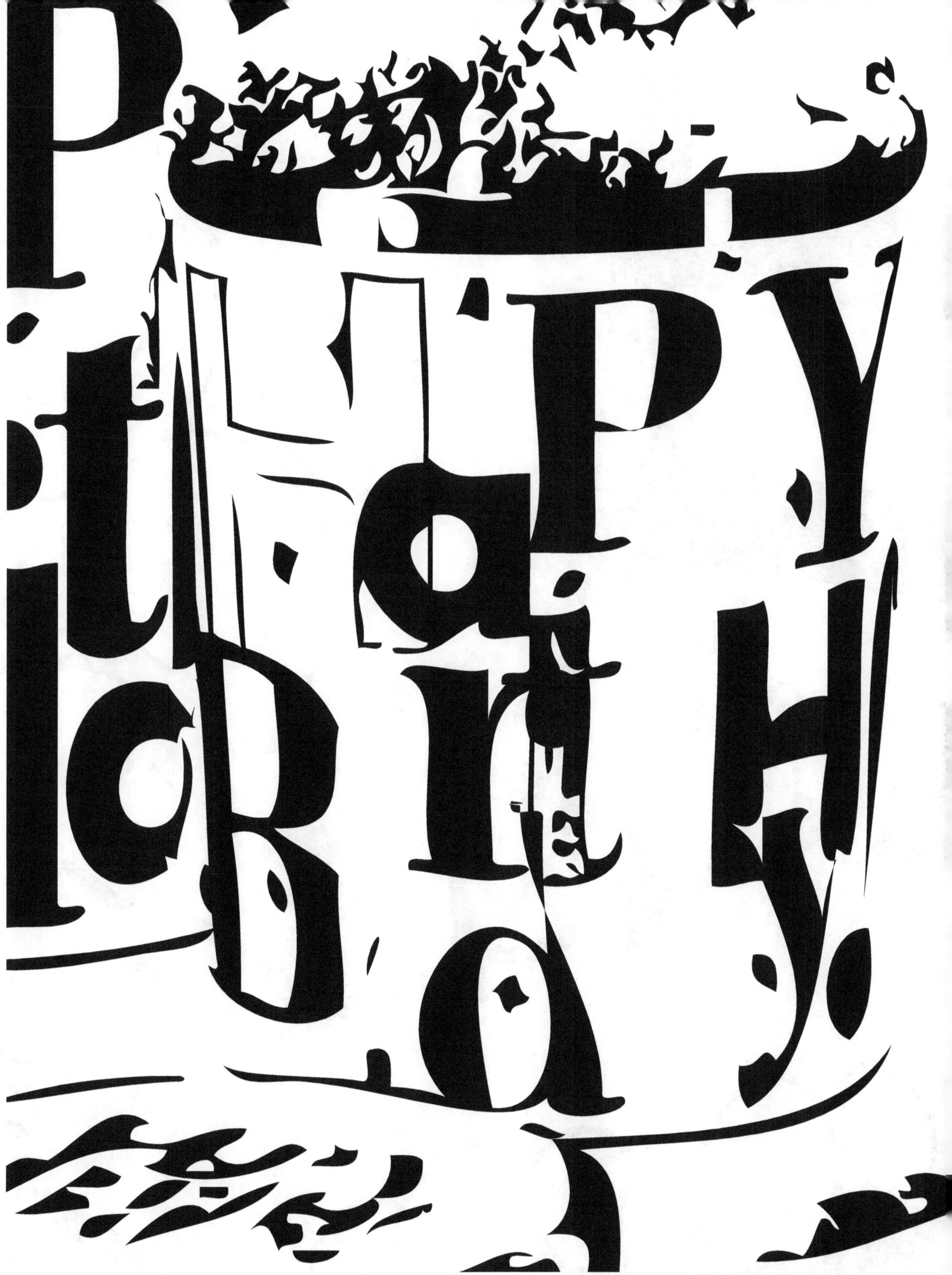

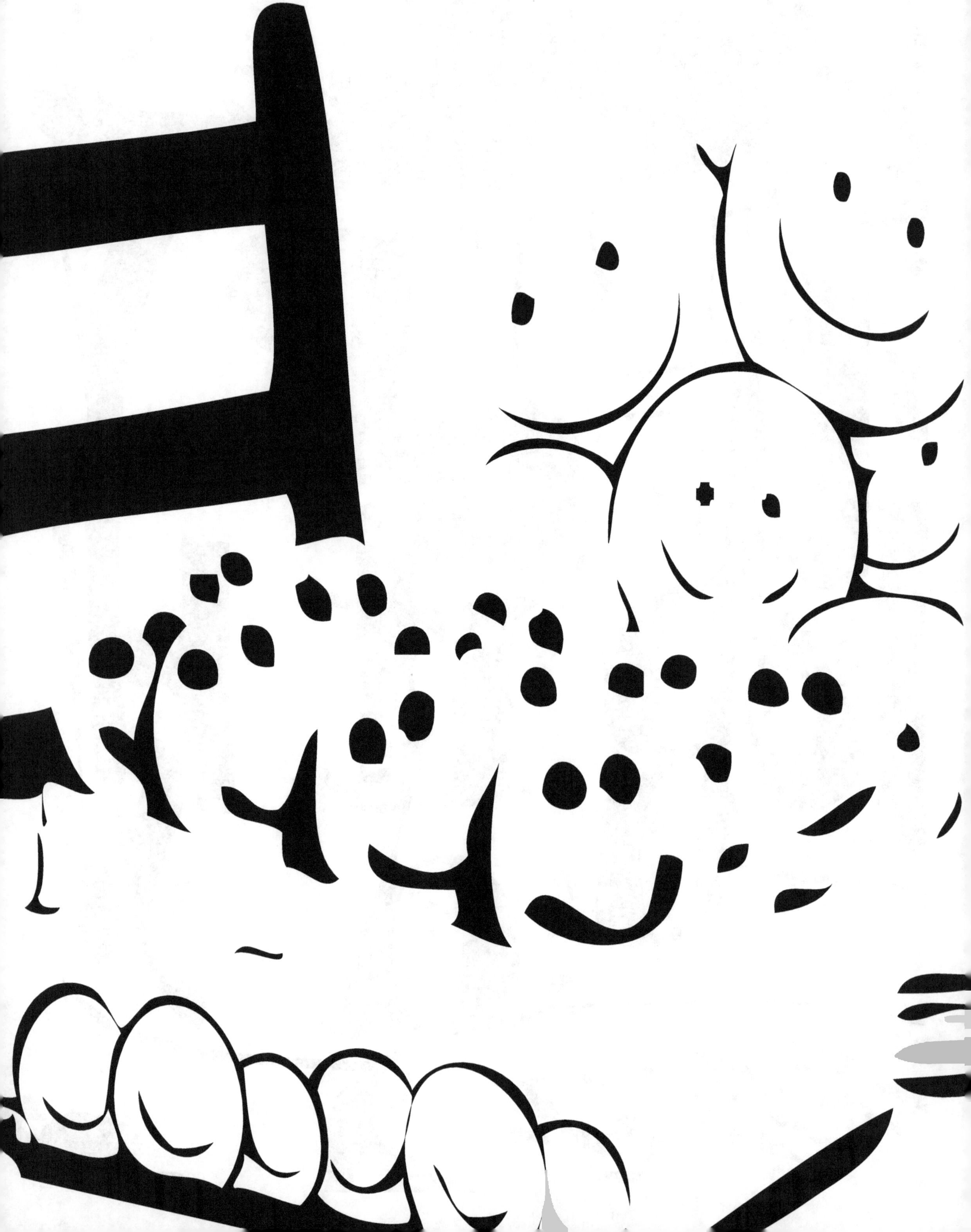

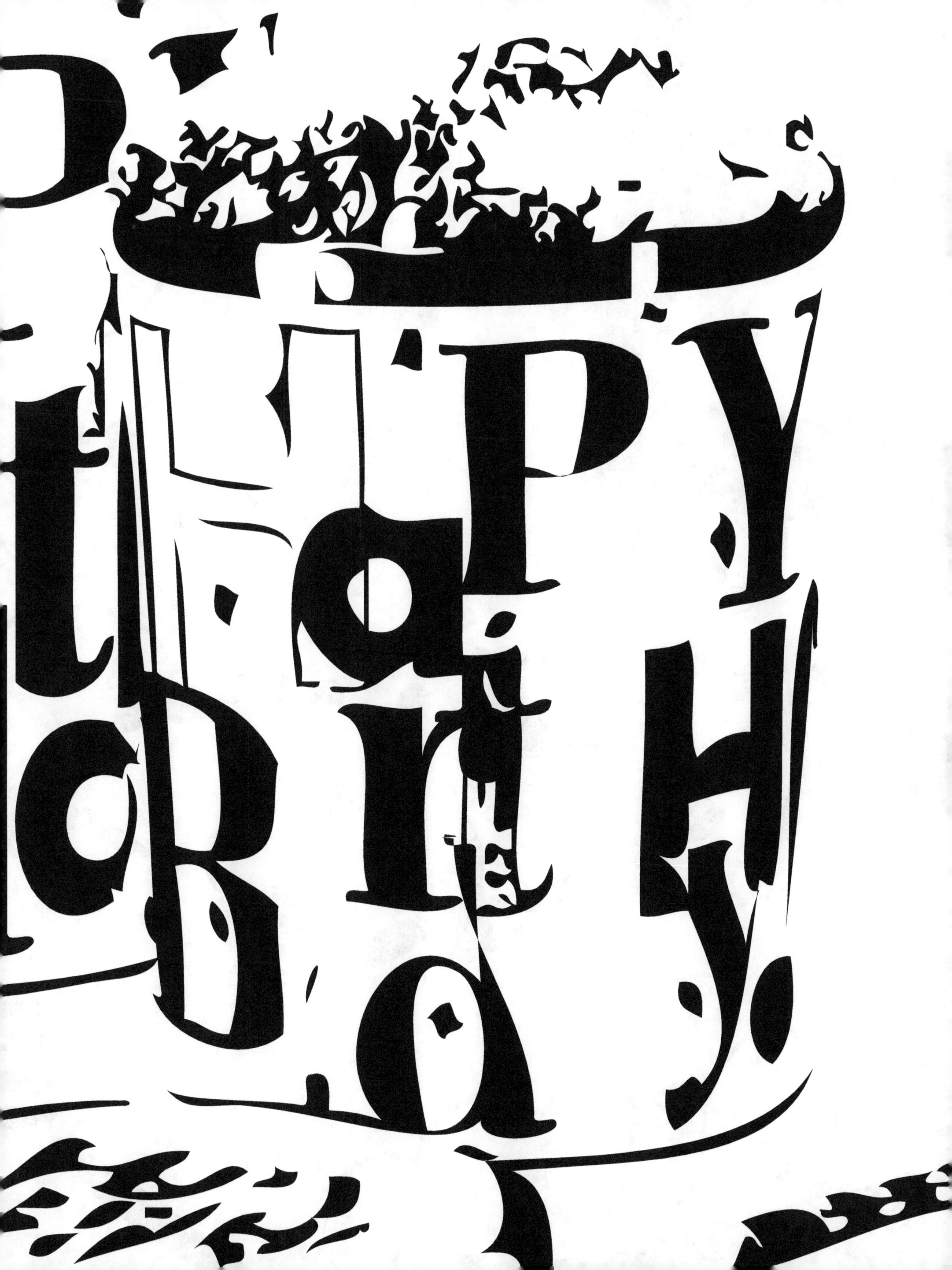

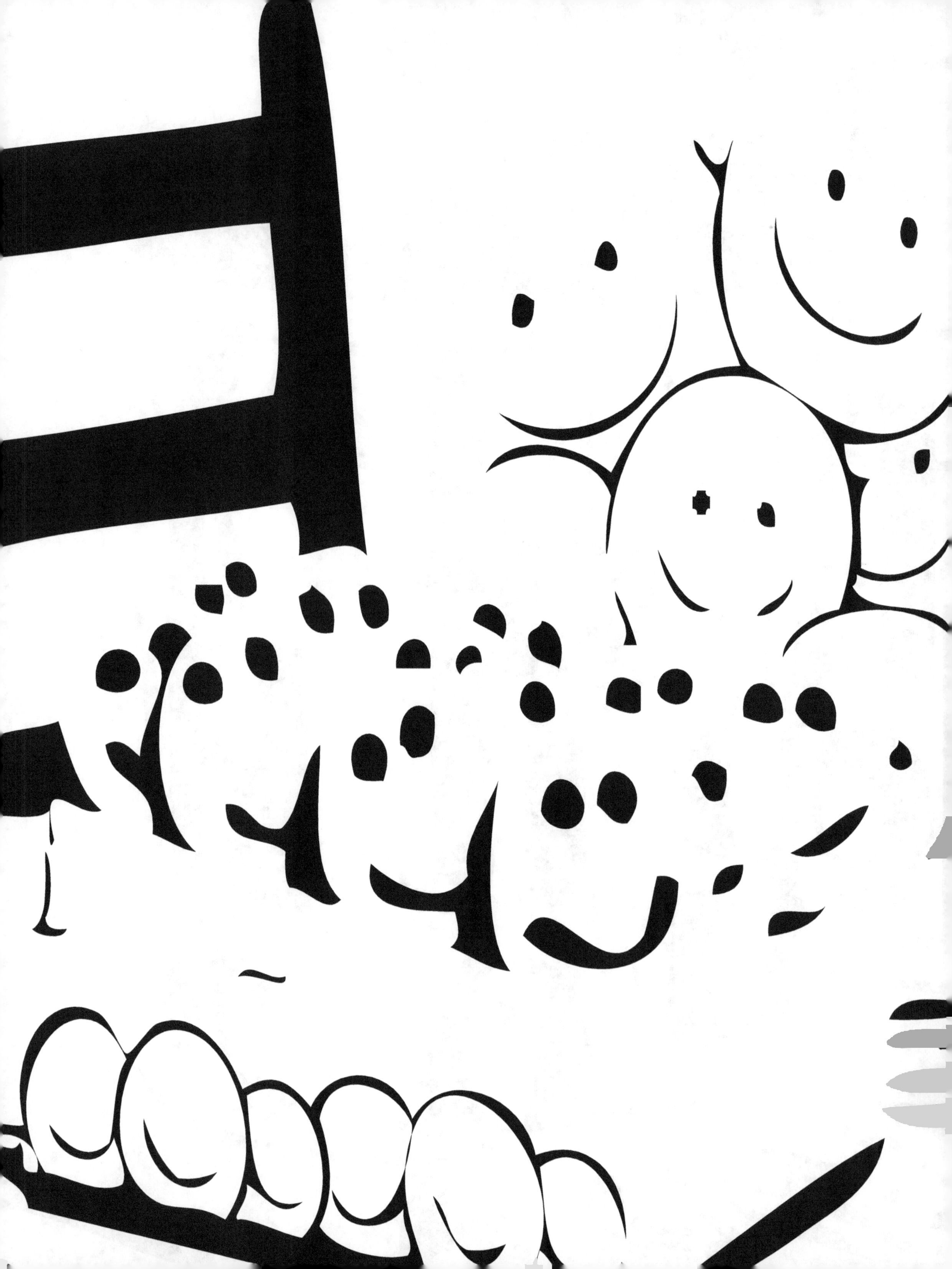

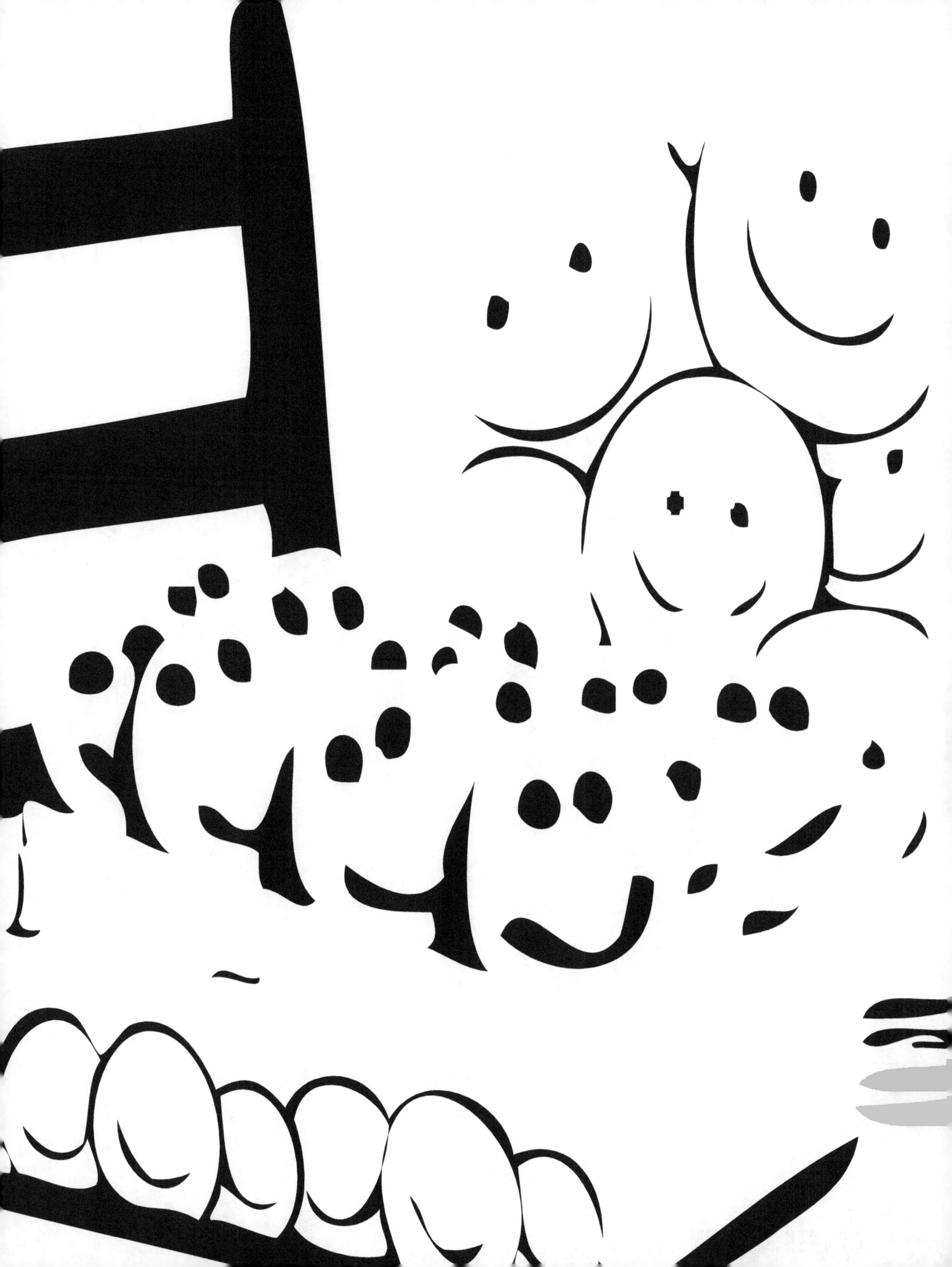

www.ingramcontent.com/pod-product-compliance
Lightning Source LLC
Chambersburg PA
CBHW080623180526
45168CB00007B/3029
* 9 7 8 1 5 1 7 2 1 9 6 7 3 *